Here's to You!

Also by Florence Isaacs

Just a Note to Say . . .
Business Notes
My Deepest Sympathies

Here's to You!

CREATING YOUR OWN

MEANINGFUL TOAST OR TRIBUTE

FOR ANY OCCASION

FLORENCE ISAACS

CLARKSON POTTER/PUBLISHERS
NEW YORK

Published by Clarkson Potter/Publishers, New York, New York.
Member of the Crown Publishing Group, a division of Random House, Inc.
www.randomhouse.com

CLARKSON N. POTTER is a trademark and POTTER and colophon
are registered trademarks of Random House, Inc.

Printed in the United States of America

Design by Jan Derevjanik

Library of Congress Cataloging-in-Publication Data
Isaacs, Florence.
Here's to you! creating your own meaningful toast or
tribute for any occasion / Florence Isaacs.
1. Toasts.   I. Title.
PN6341 .I82 2002
808.5'1—dc21   2002001821

ISBN 0-609-60919-X

10 9 8 7 6 5 4 3

First Edition

To the men in my life:

Harvey, Andrew, and Jonathan

acknowledgments

So many people generously shared their words and experiences with me that it is impossible to thank them all. I do wish to single out a few, however.

The insights and contributions of Rhonda Barad and Donn Avallone were enormously helpful to me, especially at the beginning of this project.

Minda Zetlin got married at just the right time to provide me with material. She and Harvey Hoffman led me to other important resources. Eleanor Margolies, a talented poet, helped enormously, as did Jason Frisch, Sarah Blevins and her family, Christina Page, and Barbara Turkington. I also thank Gail Brunje and the entire birthday party gang. You know who you are.

This book wouldn't have happened without you.

contents

✂

part three

BUSINESS AND
PROFESSIONAL OCCASIONS

introduction

Chances are you'll never have to toast the winner of the Nobel Peace Prize, the Swiss ambassador to the United States, or the latest inductee to the Football Hall of Fame. But in the course of daily life, there are plenty of personal occasions when you may wish to say a few words. You may be celebrating someone's promotion, marking a colleague's retirement, or praising the winner of the Teacher of the Year award. You may be the best man at a wedding, expected to toast the bride and groom, or you might find yourself raising a glass at your father's milestone birthday celebration. At times like these, sincere words of admiration, affection, or acknowledgment touch honorees and audiences alike.

Although we love toasts, the prospect of delivering them can be daunting. You don't want to bore people, speak in clichés, or sound like a dolt—and you needn't. Armed with the tips and techniques that follow, you can find meaningful words for any occasion—intelligent, compelling tributes at business or professional events, caring and meaningful toasts at family gatherings and other social occasions. And as you will see, you don't have to be an orator or stage star to do it. You just have to follow some easy guidelines and be yourself.

WHY TOAST?

A toast is the act of raising a glass and drinking in honor of someone or something, but it can also be a *proposal* to do so, or the speech given before taking such a drink. Since antiquity, toasting has been a way to express connection, friendship, and kinship. Its origins trace back to ancient religious ceremonies, when mortals used libations to offer thanks to the gods. Over time, the practice evolved into toasts to people. A toast became a way to wish someone good health or good fortune in an undertaking. The word *toast* comes from the Latin word *tostus*, meaning "a piece of bread." Toasted over a flame, the bread was added to the wine, supposedly improving the taste.

Today, a toast represents a chance to do more than just voice good wishes, and there is more to it than is generally realized. A toast is a way to create ambience, making any event memorable; it also creates a bond between the honoree and the audience, loosening everyone up and serving as a great conversation starter. When we toast, we affirm others with sentiments that so often go unexpressed—love, respect, pride. People tend to bask in the glow of this attention.

A toast is special because it tends to be a public statement to the world at large. Raise a glass, say some words of recognition to an associate, or to the nephew who got accepted at medical school, and you speak volumes about your regard for him. At the same time, you also implicitly say something positive about yourself, because you made a gracious effort.

Toasting can also be a way to recognize friends for their understanding or loyalty, to thank customers for sending business your way, or to applaud employees for effort above and beyond. It needn't be limited to formal occasions. Did you and your family spend a wonderful weekend at somebody's country house? A toast at dinner might go, "We've had the best time, and you've been the perfect hosts. Thank you from all of us for your special hospitality. To Lynn and Walter." An even shorter version might be, "Here's to Lynn and Walter. We don't want to go home!" Nothing fancy, but exactly what hosts want to hear.

But you don't have to drink to recognize someone; in fact, on many occasions, drinking is not appropriate. A *toast* always involves raising a glass, usually includes words such as "To Ann and Victor," and tends to be brief. A *tribute*, on the other hand, is a longer testimonial that provides details of someone's admirable qualities or accomplishments. A tribute can be (and often is) included in a toast, as in the case of a twenty-fifth wedding anniversary. You will probably toast the couple, but you may also give a longer tribute to their relationship.

It's also possible to connect and communicate with a more formal tribute that stands alone. You may, for example, be called upon to praise the guest of honor at a community or charity event, the recipient of an industry award, or the outgoing president of the PTA. On occasions like these, there won't be any clinking of champagne glasses, but you can still make your remarks meaningful and heartfelt.

Whether professional or personal, whether carefully scripted or impromptu, toasts and tributes offer an opportunity to publicly recognize the people you care about and respect. Whatever the occasion, this book will help you to speak warm, meaningful words every time.

essential know-how

ONE

MEANINGFUL WORDS FOR
THE 21ST CENTURY

$\mathcal{M}$y husband never had a real birthday party as a child; at best, someone stuck a candle in a cake. That's why parties have always been important to him as an adult. It was not at all surprising, then, that Harvey decided to throw himself the ultimate celebration for a recent milestone birthday. Determined to make it a magical experience, he planned to hold the event in the Champagne region of France. Faxes flew back and forth to likely restaurant locations for months until he finally made his choice. Then he focused on selecting the perfect menu, not leaving a single detail to chance.

When the big day finally arrived, our family and friends gathered at the elegant restaurant Harvey had chosen. It was located in a turn-of-the-century mansion on a park-like estate, the sort of place seen only in your dreams or in the movies.

The evening began with champagne cocktails on a terrace overlooking sprawling lawns and plantings. We later adjourned to a private dining room fit for royalty, where hot and cold running waiters served a six-course meal, complete with appropriate wines. *(Mais oui!)*

Now, this fantastic setting would have made my husband's party a special one in any case, but what made it truly unforgettable was the human element. Weeks earlier, I had asked attendees to arrive prepared to say a few words about him, humorous or otherwise. Before dessert, they rose one after another to honor him with a variety of toasts and tributes that he will always remember.

In an evening of laughter and love, this imaginative group extolled my husband's virtues, tweaked his well-known foibles, and reminisced about their history together. Some people recalled how they first met him; others told work-related war stories. A business and personal friend said in praise, "Harvey is a valued adviser and I wouldn't be nearly as effective without his counsel. He's the firebrand; I'm the quiet guy. He makes working in the industry a pleasure." Then, to top it off, one quartet harmonized a song to the tune of "Harrigan" that celebrated Harvey's skills as an attorney:

> *H-a-r-v-e-y,*
> *That spells our friend, Harvey;*

Proud of all accomplishments you've garnered,
Among your loving friends, you're being honored.

Flo, Andrew, Jonathan, too,
You're a marvelous crew.

You've got a name, legal fame;
Ever more is connected with
Harvey, that's you!

In a joyous night that became a treasured memory, my husband—along with the rest of us—laughed and cried.

It's no wonder that these songs and short speeches meant so much to my husband. He *wanted* to be remembered and appreciated on his birthday, as we all do.

It amazed him that so many people were willing to take the time and spend the money to join him, often reorganizing vacation plans to make it possible. "That alone made it memorable," he recalls. "As anticipated, the meal was 'to die for,' but the toasts made by everyone were unforgettable, up to and including the childhood memories of my sons. There was nothing that I would change."

Harvey adored being feted by close friends and family—and *they* loved participating in the event, too. Instead of freezing or growing self-conscious, everyone made an effort to say things that were personal, meaningful, and true. Allowing themselves to become a bit vulnerable, they reached within to express affection and admiration, emotions that frequently get swept aside in the course of our busy lives.

Of course, birthdays are just one of many social occasions that allow us to reaffirm ties with those we care about. As we're increasingly squeezed for time to relax and be ourselves with people important to us, celebrations help us get back in touch with our humanity. They're a chance to reinforce bonds that bring meaning to our lives and reconnect with who we are.

In your business and professional life, situations when you're required to say a few words offer opportunities, too. The best toasts and tributes are about relationships. They create community and connections with customers, associates, employees, and others who have an impact on your career or work life. They raise your professional visibility, as well as the visibility of the person you're toasting.

At such times, however, it's natural to fear that you will sound foolish or will flounder about for words. It's common to hear, "I hate giving toasts, because it's always so embarrassing," or, "When I have to give a toast, I never know what to say." Indeed, your choice of words does say a lot about you, but never fear—it's easy to find something significant to say when you have the right tools at your disposal.

There's really nothing mysterious about good toasts or tributes. The best ones are customized to the individual and the event, not copied from generic models. What always works is simplicity, sincerity, and your own "take" on what's going on. Your perspective is unique, and so are your personality and your relationship with the individual. We all know people in different ways, and others *want* to hear your observations.

The challenge is to cut through the anxiety and figure out what to say. Although it is true that some people are born speakers who always seem to have the right words at their fingertips, the rest of us need some help. It's easy once you know what to do, though! Use this book to educate yourself and learn the skills to compose effective, powerful remarks. Tips, techniques, and illustrations will help you relax, trust what you know and feel, and resist the urge to censor yourself. They will inspire you, trigger ideas, and help you tap into your spontaneity in new ways.

This book is a tool you can always lean on. Pull it out for any occasion and trust it to lead you in the right direction.

TWO

BASIC TRAINING

*M*eaningful toasts and tributes are not about drinking songs, nor are they about clever words tripping off the tongue. In fact, too much cleverness tends to throw the spotlight on the speaker and his skill rather than on the person being celebrated. Good toasts say something that makes sense in the context of the honoree, the setting, and the circumstances, while establishing rapport with the audience. To say what matters anywhere, anytime, you need only remember a few key principles.

PERSONALIZE—TELL WHAT'S SPECIAL ABOUT THE HONOREE

At a minimum, mention the person's name and acknowledge the occasion. Take a positive approach, as in, "Bob, you always try to hide the fact that you're a softie with your tough veneer, but you never say no to a person in need. This is a big birthday for a guy with a big heart. I wish you happiness and health in the years ahead. Here's to you."

To make your own personalized toast, consider the person's trademark qualities. Is he known for his wit? Drive? Integrity? Caring? To build a connection between the honoree and the audience, you want to capture spirit and character, as in, "Ann is cranky and always speaks her mind, which is usually ten steps ahead of everyone else's." Or, "Penny is funny, smart, and thoughtful. She supports her friends in the best times and in the worst times." Or, "Mike is unpredictable in the best sense of the word. He's a fountain of ideas. Instead of resisting change, he welcomes it and rides it. He inspires the rest of us to do the same."

FACTOR IN YOUR RELATIONSHIP TO THE HONOREE

What you say to your Aunt Marie will vary from what you say to your colleague, boss, or employee. The whole tone is different. Your feelings about the person and occasion are different. You can get as emotional or silly as you want with family and friends because they know and love you, warts and all. When you're giving a toast in a room full of the people closest to you, you can spout sincere sentimentalities like, "I love you, Uncle Dave. You're the sweetest, most accepting man I've ever known," without seeming too sappy.

On the other hand, you want to sound more dignified when speaking at a formal professional function. Your words will reflect your intelligence, good taste, and judgment (or lack thereof). Positive feelings do have a place here, as in, "Your support all these years has meant everything to me." Yet you don't want to gush or sound saccharine, which only irritates everyone and may sound insincere.

REFLECT ON THE MEANING OF THE EVENT

Then make connections. A milestone birthday is a transition when you can speak to a life lived so far—and to the future. A wedding is the start of a journey together, so you might explore why the bride and groom seem so right for each other. An award honors someone's significant achievement or contribution. You can talk about the person's influence on others' lives, as in, "As a teacher, you've given so many students something to aspire to."

TARGET THE AUDIENCE

Who are these people? Family and friends? Associates who are familiar with the honoree only in the workplace? Strangers? When the audience doesn't know much about the honoree, it's up to you to supply background. Use details to humanize the person, as in, "Helen got where she is because she's a legal wizard, but she's also someone with eclectic interests. Few realize that she's an authority on doo-wop." Such contrasts intrigue people, who tend to smile, turn to each other, and say, "I didn't know that. Did you?"

The audience counts when using jargon as well. Are you addressing colleagues who will understand it—or spouses and people in other fields who will not? Remember, you want to communicate, not obfuscate.

Factor in audience size, too. A formal speech is appropriate at a banquet for five hundred. But you can pass around a photo album for show-and-tell at an office party or a family gathering.

Finally, it can also be fun to toast in another language. Try "A votre santé" (French) or, depending on the background of the honoree or audience, "L'Chayim" (Yiddish).

CONSIDER THE TONE
OF THE OCCASION

Is it casual—a gathering of your department in the lunchroom, a birthday party in a finished basement—or is it a ballroom dinner dance? For informal family occasions and the company picnic, people often get playful. To celebrate the birth of a baby or forty years on the job, they might compose a poem or set their own words to a popular tune. If the occasion suits it and you're in the mood, poems or songs can be a wonderful way to add fun to the festivities.

INCLUDE MEMORIES AND ANECDOTES

Your personal recollections of the honoree are powerful, whether you recount how your sister took you to your first Broadway play, how your brother taught you to play chess, or how your coworker praised you to your boss. Such defining moments touch everyone; sharing your experiences links you and the honoree with the audience.

You can also hold attention and add interest with grander anecdotes, such as how the honoree rebuilt his company after a devastating fire destroyed the building. Ask yourself: What is this person's greatest accomplishment, and how does it reflect his character?

TRY QUOTES

They can energize your tribute, *if* you choose them with care. You must be able to genuinely tie them in to the person or issue; they must be pertinent and illustrate a point you want to make. Too often, people pick out a quotation by a poet, politician, or celebrity that has no connection with what is going on. Such quotes simply confuse and distance the audience. You really do need a scalpel here.

For example, "Love is an excuse for its own faults" is an Italian proverb that is guaranteed to have everyone at a wedding groaning. The response is likely to be, "Huh? So what?" On the other hand, the following quote really worked in a business tribute: "*Dabit qui dedit* is Latin for 'He who has given will give.' As a fund-raiser extraordinaire, Patricia understands it well. She consistently persuades generous contributors to up the ante even more."

USE FACTS AND STATISTICS

On September 14, 1962, President John F. Kennedy made a stirring tribute to the Australian and U.S. crews at the America's Cup race. In the speech at a dinner given by the Australian ambassador in Newport, Rhode Island, President Kennedy mused about our connection to the sea, tying in a little-known fact of biology. He said in part:

> *I really don't know why it is that all of us are so committed to the sea, except I think it is because in addition to the fact that the sea changes and the light changes, and ships change, it is because we all came from the sea. And it is an interesting biological fact that all of us have, in our veins, the exact same percentage of salt in our blood that exists in the ocean, and therefore, we have salt in our blood, in our sweat, in our tears.*
>
> *We are tied to the ocean. And when we go back to the sea, whether it is to sail or to watch it, we are going back from whence we came.*
>
> *Therefore, it is quite natural that the United States and Australia, separated by an ocean, but particularly those of us who regard the ocean as a friend, bound by an ocean, should be meeting today in Newport to begin this great sea competition.*

The factual information about salt adds an "I didn't know that" quality, and is one reason Kennedy's words remain unforgettable today. They enlighten, inspire, and connect us.

For relevant statistics and other information you can use, check newspapers and other publications such as *The Wall Street Journal* (especially the front page) and *American Demographics* magazine. Save clips that strike your interest in a file folder for future use. A toast to someone leaving your department might say, "I just read that four million Americans change jobs every month. But none of them will be missed as much as you. To Aaron."

COMPOSING YOUR MESSAGE

Brief is usually best for a toast, and one minute or less is ideal in most cases. You will find there's a lot you can say in sixty seconds. On occasions when you want to make a more elaborate statement, do so, but avoid anything longer than three to five minutes. You don't want to chill the audience. One of the nicest toasts I can think of, applicable for weddings (and adaptable for anniversaries and birthdays), is essentially two words: "To Bill and Amy: Be happy."

A tribute, which doesn't involve raising a glass, is usually longer than a toast. It can run anywhere from one to (in rare instances) fifteen minutes, depending on who you are, your expertise as a speaker, the occasion, and the honoree. In many cases, you will be told how long to speak. When in doubt, err on the side of brevity. Have you ever heard anyone lament, "That speech was too short"?

Even if you plan a one-sentence toast, think it through. For something longer, after you've done any necessary research, write it down stream-of-consciousness. Grab a pad of paper, stretch out leisurely on a couch or in a comfortable chair, and start scribbling. You'll be surprised at what tumbles out.

If you prefer, you can brainstorm by speaking into a tape recorder. The point is that you want to free yourself up to plumb true insights and articulate your feelings about the person and event. Once you've gotten everything out, you can then start editing and organizing.

As you rewrite and polish, eliminate words that clutter up what you're saying. Instead of "in his capacity of chairman," just say "as chairman." Use specific details to strengthen your point. Say, "He doubled sales," rather than the general "He increased business." Use a thesaurus to search for fresh words and avoid repeating the same ones in the same sentence or two. Resist those clichés, and speak conversationally. You want to sound like yourself.

OPENINGS AND CLOSINGS

When opening, remember that you want to capture everyone's attention. Begin with an unexpected bit of information, a great quote, or a funny joke or anecdote. Then, make it relevant. A testimonial to the retiring president of a St. Louis company started with an arresting statement, and got to the point fast: "In the world of business, there are three kinds of people—the finders, the minders, and the grinders. The finders bring in new accounts. The minders manage them, and the grinders do the day-to-day work. You've always been an extraordinary finder, Tom, which is one of the many reasons why you'll be missed."

An article about the automobile industry inspired this opening in a tribute to someone celebrating twenty-five years with the same company: "They've retired the Oldsmobile. The Edsel and DeLorean are gone. But Frank is still here—charged with fresh ideas and exciting projects."

A toast to a real estate broker began, "Here's to Marty! Twenty million homes in the United States have an acre of land or more, and he seems to have sold most of them."

Lift your closings, as well, with an appropriate anecdote or quote from the honoree (or about him or her). One speech concluded, "Just last week a young researcher told me, 'I wouldn't be here without Mike. He gave me my start.' He's given that and more to an entire generation of scientists and to all Americans. Join me in saluting Mike Callaghan."

President Kennedy closed his America's Cup speech with these rousing words: "I want to toast tonight the crew, the sailors, those who made it possible for the *Gretel* to come here, those who have, for a hundred years, defended this Cup from the New York Yacht Club, to all of them. As the Ambassador said so well, they race against each other, but they also race *with* each other against the wind—and the sea. To the crew of the *Gretel* and the crew of the *Weatherly*."

DELIVERY

The way you deliver the speech counts. You can ruin a good anecdote with the wrong intonation at the wrong time. You don't want to stumble through either, but it's easy to learn the skills to give a "good-enough" performance.

Here are some ways to reduce the anxiety that usually accompanies public speaking.

REHEARSE AGAIN AND AGAIN

Say it out loud so you can hear whether it sounds natural and real. Watch the "uhs" that tend to creep in; awareness reduces their frequency. When you're talking to family and friends you don't have to worry so much. They're not expecting Billy Crystal.

Recording your words can help, too. To imprint the material in her memory, a friend of mine tapes the speech, then plays it while wrapping Christmas gifts or peeling potatoes.

WRITE IT OUT ON CARDS OR PAPER

Although rehearsal will empower you and improve your performance, it's still important to compose a bulleted outline or, if you prefer, work from notes. Writing down even a two-line toast is a good idea. Although you may not have to refer to it, it's there if you need to glance at it. Then you don't have to worry about going blank.

NEVER PUT YOURSELF DOWN

Don't tell the audience you don't know what to say. Never say, "I'm nervous," or, "I can't imagine why I was chosen to speak because I'm not good at it," or anything else self-deprecating. Be confident. The audience assumes that you are competent, so why call their attention to your deficits and shoot yourself in the foot?

USE COMMON SENSE ABOUT HUMOR

As one executive told me, "Less is more. Don't try to be what you're not. If you're not a comedian, don't try to imitate one." Nothing is more leaden than a quip that's meant to be funny but isn't. For an objective view of how you come across, bounce your remarks off a few colleagues or family members whose judgment you trust. One man always uses his wife as a sounding board. "She protects me from myself," he explains.

AD LIB AT YOUR OWN RISK

You might wind up saying something damaging! A funny colleague of mine who often makes toasts was once asked, "Do you prepare these remarks or do you ad lib them?" His reply, "I ad lib them—several hours earlier. I like knowing what I'm going to say and how I'm going to begin and end." Beware of talking about a subject outside your area, too. It's all too easy to err.

CHECK OUT THE ROOM IN ADVANCE

Familiarize yourself with the environment in which you'll speak. Walk up to the podium and imagine the audience before you. Stroll around the room and get comfortable with it. This simple preparation will help you feel more confident. To avoid surprises, check the microphone and make sure it's in working order.

When you care about what you're saying, it comes across— and *that's* what's important. If you wish to improve your speaking skills, however, consider joining Toastmasters International. Call 1-800-993-7732 for the location of a club in your area, or check out their website at http://www.toastmasters.org.

TOASTING ETIQUETTE

The timing is pretty much up to you. You can toast a guest of honor at the start of a meal, before the main course, or at dessert. At a cocktail party, many people arrive late; others leave early. To reach the largest audience at an event scheduled for, say, six to eight o'clock, make your toast around seven o'clock. That's when most guests are likely to be present.

Who proposes a toast varies. At an informal dinner, anyone can do it. At a business-related event, the host toasts the honoree first, and he may be the sole toaster. If you want to make a toast yourself, but the host hasn't made his move, you can ask whether he'd mind if you said a few words.

At a formal occasion, a toastmaster may preside. His job is to propose or announce toasts and introduce speakers. The toastmaster may be one of the hosts or he may be hired for the event.

Back in ancient Rome, incidentally, a toastmaster had a different function. He kept tabs on how much wine people drank at festivities, and whether the wine was watered down. In those days, full-strength wine was frowned upon.

You can toast with champagne, wine, or any beverage at all, depending on the occasion and your preference. If the choice is champagne, however, serve it in a flute or tulip-shaped glass to preserve the bubbles. Make sure people's glasses have been filled before you begin a toast. Click your glass with a spoon to get attention. You'd be surprised at how effective that is to quiet a noisy room and focus everyone on what you are about to say. Don't overdo it, however. Glasses have broken at the hands of the overzealous!

You don't *have* to stand to propose a toast, but it makes a more powerful statement. If there's a crowd, it also ensures you'll be heard above the din of conversation. If your group is small, however, you can remain seated. At the end of the toast, look the person square in the eye and say something like, "Here's to Henry." A toast can also be preceded by the words, "To————"; "Join me in a toast to————"; "Let's toast————"; or "Let's drink to——."

Of course, there are all kinds of reasons today why some people can't or won't drink alcohol. They may be teetotalers or recovering alcoholics; others simply cannot drink for health reasons. Regardless, don't fuss over them or treat them differently. They can join in the toast with an empty glass or a glass of water, or they can just raise an arm. As an abstaining friend of mine observes, "It's not what's in your glass, it's what's in your heart."

When you're the honoree, don't imbibe. (It's tacky to salute yourself!) Just say, "Thank you" with a gracious smile. It is proper to return the toast with very brief remarks such as, "I always said you know how to throw a party, Andy. I'll never forget this fiftieth birthday. You're a great friend and a splendid host. Thank you." You can then simply raise your glass to the host or add, "To Andy."

social situations

THREE

WEDDINGS

*W*hen most people think of toasts, they automatically think of weddings. Although the best man is the only person *required* to make a toast at the wedding reception, others close to the couple often get into the act, especially the father of the bride or the groom. Toasts are also made at the rehearsal dinner. Anything goes today, now that weddings have grown more informal and more tailored to the couple's personal tastes.

If you're going to toast, it's only natural to feel anxious. A wedding is, after all, one of the most significant events in a person's life. The bride has been dreaming about it since age six and everyone else anticipates a joyous day. In addition, you may not know many of the people in the room—all those guests from "the other side of the aisle." What's most important is to relax and realize it's okay to be human. People expect you to be nervous. What they will remember most are your genuine feelings, simply expressed.

The information that follows will help you do a good (and appropriate) job with any wedding toast.

KEEP IT SHORT

Most of us can say quite enough in one to two minutes. Three minutes should be the limit. At one outdoor wedding, the father of the groom spoke for an hour in the middle of a heat wave. Guests sweltered in 98-degree weather as he chronicled his son's accomplishments since birth.

KEEP IT POSITIVE

Avoid statements like, "We never thought Jim would settle down," and omit tales of old romances. Negative is always inappropriate. "Don't cry, either," advises one recent groom. "It's icky. No one wants to be manipulated."

Of course, the ultimate best-man fiasco takes place in the movie *Four Weddings and a Funeral.* In one hilarious scene, Hugh Grant's character rises to toast the bride and groom and ends up shocking the wedding guests with a story of the last time he was a best man. He tells a hushed audience that the couple is now divorced—the groom cheated on his new wife with her sister *and* her mother!

This disastrous toast ends on a positive note, though, when he finally begins to focus on the couple at hand. Expressing his sincere wonder at the commitment the two have made to each other, he admits that he himself couldn't make such an emotional investment. He then asks the guests to raise their glasses "to the adorable couple."

LISTEN TO YOUR HEART

A wedding stirs all kinds of emotions in the couple's friends and relatives, so, how does this wedding make *you* feel? Thrilled at seeing two people so happy? Then say so. It's sincerity, not polish, that makes a toast memorable. Mentioning in your toast how you're feeling can create a real bond between you and your audience.

REALIZE THIS IS NOT ABOUT *YOU*

It's about the bride and groom. Do not ramble on about how nervous you are or anything else about yourself unless it relates directly to the couple. This is their day. At one wedding, a misguided friend of the groom spoke for forty-five minutes about his own life and his wife and children. He was so annoying that some guests finally started loud conversations to drown him out.

Do tell the audience who you are, however. Not everyone there knows you, and it heads off the buzz of guests turning to each other to ask, "Is he the groom's brother?" A short introduction and a small amount of background information about yourself can eliminate a lot of unnecessary confusion. Just remember not to overdo it. The two people who really matter at the wedding are the bride and groom!

CENSOR YOUR HUMOR

Just because you've known the groom since both of you were in diapers does not give you license to make off-color comments. You can be funny if you wish, without being offensive. Other guests *are* present.

CONSIDER THE CIRCUMSTANCES

One-third of all marriages are remarriages, according to Hallmark. If it's a second or even a third marriage, you can mention in your toast that this is another chance at happiness, if you wish. You can also phrase it this way: "If there were ever two people who are perfect together, it's the two of you. It took you awhile, but you're where you belong."

If the couple is already living together, remember that the wedding is still very special to them—and everyone else in the family. It announces to the world their commitment to each other. One toaster took a light approach for a couple who had lived together for five years before the wedding: "Well, it's about time! It's great to see you finally taking the plunge. To Jill and Joe—health and happiness always."

Of course, the specifics of your toast will vary, depending on your relationship with the bride and groom and your role in the wedding. Here are a few ways to search your memory and say something particularly special.

BEST-MAN TOASTS

Make your toast at the reception after everyone is seated. Remember, you're in this role because you're very close to the groom. Talk about him and that relationship, and include some comment about the bride or the couple, as the following toast does so well:

> *About eleven years ago I met the best friend anyone could ever ask for—Jon.*
>
> *About five months ago, Jon asked me to be his best man, the greatest honor a friend can bestow.*
>
> *About one hour ago, I witnessed a perfect beginning to the rest of Jon's life as he placed a ring on Jamie's finger.*
>
> *Jon's impact on me as a roommate, fraternity brother, business associate—and, most important, as my best friend—will last forever. It all began one frightful day in our freshman year at Tulane University. I say "frightful" because he has not been able to get rid of me since.*

We lived together for four years during college, becoming as close as brothers. Our relationship grew even stronger when we returned to New York and we guided each other through the perils of careers on Wall Street. We are more than best friends today. Jon is my most trusted adviser and confidant.

Jon and Jamie's happiness together leads me to believe that we are brought into this world, each as part of a puzzle (preferably a corner piece). With every day that passes we find a new piece to add to our person. And eventually we begin to see a picture of the lives we've created.

But as with many puzzles, we wait to find that last piece that fits right in the center of our being and makes us complete. Jon and Jamie are lucky. They each found the one person that made everything fit. Tonight, you both, as one, begin a new puzzle. Your rings are two corners, your vows are two corners, and your love for one another will guide you through the rest.

I realize that Jon now has a new best friend. But Jon, Jamie won't sit with you on your couch on Sundays watching football and eating buffalo wings— so I know there will still be room for me.

On a closing and serious note, Jon and I did a lot of growing up together. Now, Jon and Jamie, you will spend the rest of your lives growing your world together. This is your night to shine—and you do. I love you both. Cheers.

The toast not only honored the *couple*, but touched upon the issue of whether the friends' relationship would now change. It's only human to wonder about that. Such feelings strike a chord in us all, and you can use them to make your toast powerful and poignant.

Another best man philosophized on friendship with these words from the heart:

With this toast I wanted to find a way to express what it means to have such a good friend your whole life. As I thought about that, I realized that I don't have many memories older than my friendship with Jeff. Knowing that my friend has now found a wife who is a friend and lover too is what makes standing up here such an honor. Knowing that for the rest of his life my friend will have somebody to share with, to count on, to live with, to live for, and to love.

That is what friendships that last a lifetime mean to me. So here is to love and luck and friendships that last a lifetime.

In a funny yet loving speech at his younger brother's wedding, another best man gave advice to both the bride and groom:

Most best man's speeches start off by telling an embarrassing story about the groom. I thought about doing this, as well, but figured it was Matthew and he would embarrass himself enough on his own.

Being married myself for two years, I will bestow what little knowledge I have on this subject.

Matthew, I give this advice to you:

Always put the toilet seat down.

If you ever have children, never utter these words to your pregnant wife: "Wow, you really can't see your feet!"

And finally, remember that a single rose from the heart means more than a dozen roses every day.

Faith, I give this advice to you:

Make sure Matthew keeps his zany sense of humor.

Don't forget, Matthew has the ability to move mountains when he puts his mind to it. He once built an airplane from scratch. Granted, it never got off the ground, but just imagine what he could do with a paintbrush when the house needs painting!

And, every once in a while, get Matthew to stop planning for the future and enjoy the present. Matthew probably couldn't tell us what he had for lunch today, but he can definitely tell us what he'll be doing in five years. Together you should enjoy each day as it comes, and the future will fall into place.

With that said, let us raise our glasses to this beautiful bride and this handsome groom, and may happiness come to them from this day forward.

This brief toast focused on the couple: "Since Bill met Debbie, I've felt that I'm getting two for the price of one. I've never seen two people so right together. They complete one another. They are soulmates. Their relationship is a model of what marriage should be for my generation."

Another best man spoke to what was going on in the couple's life (they had just bought a new house and a new van together) and kidded the groom, an accountant, about how he had changed:

> *I've known Joe for many years and he always said that someday he planned to be a rich man. And there were three things he would never do. First he would never buy a new car . . . how's that van of yours, Joe? Second, he would never borrow a large sum of money . . . and how are you doing with those mortgage payments? Third, he would never get married . . . how's that ring feeling on your finger? Joe, the promise you made today is what will make you a rich man.*

PARENT TOASTS

Parents of the bride and groom may also wish to toast the couple. In this case, you can reminisce about your child and philosophize about what a son or daughter means, as in: "To a father, a daughter is a precious jewel. Cindy is my treasure and it's an emotional thing to see her start a new life with the man she loves. Love her well, Jim. She's my little girl, and she's in your care. To Cindy and Jim—happiness and love."

Be sure to remember the new spouse. In one case a father of the bride extolled his daughter and her sister, the maid of honor, but never even mentioned the groom!

Another parent asked, "What do we want for our children? Above all, happiness. I feel blessed to be able to say that Jonas and Elise have found it together. To them both."

If you yourself have a good marriage, you can talk about that, as in, "Your mother and I have built a wonderful, satisfying marriage over the thirty-seven years we've been together. The inevitable ups and downs have only made it stronger. I wish that same love, loyalty, and strength for the two of you."

This toast by a father of the bride took the form of a thank-you to the groom: "Thank you, Martin, for making Karen so happy—and for becoming part of our family. May you both live a long, happy, and (relatively) normal life, and may you grow old together." Such warm words really help welcome a new son-in-law into the family.

You can also put it this way: "We're thrilled that you are becoming a permanent member of the Jones clan. It's about time we had a computer guru in the family."

Think about how much the bride and groom have in common. Then you can say something like, "They're both neat. They love film noir, Mexican food, and baseball. And they're passionate Democrats. Perfect match! To Lilly and Doug, and to their happiness-filled future!"

If they're not alike, just discuss how different they are, yet how good they are together. As the saying goes, sometimes opposites really do attract. You'll have everyone laughing if you make jokes about the very different personalities of an "odd couple."

One father of the bride added a bit of showmanship to his toast, announcing, "And now I have some advice for the bride and groom." He called the couple to the front of the room and whispered in their ears. Then the bride and groom returned to their seats.

"It was great. Nobody knew what he said, and everyone wondered," recalls the bride. What did he say? "Don't take advice from anyone."

Stepparents can toast, too. One stepfather said in his toast, "I feel all the love in the room for Doris and Lowell, these two marvelous young people. It isn't surprising. Who doesn't melt at their happiness? You know it's true that Doris is my stepdaughter. But I couldn't love her more if she was my own. I've considered her my daughter for many years." He then went on to speak of how close he felt to the bride. There wasn't a dry eye in the place.

If the father of the groom makes a toast, he toasts the bride. Someone did it this way: "Rachel, I am thrilled that my son has found someone so wonderful to share his life with. What a lucky man he is—and how fortunate *I* am. To Rachel."

A mother of the groom toasted:

I've waited a long time for this day and it makes my heart sing to be here. First let me say that like his mother, Rob has always been a late bloomer. He took longer than many to decide what he wanted to do with his life—and to find the girl of his dreams. But he did find her—and she's a honey. I am blessed with Rita. Now I have the daughter I've always wanted. I love you both so much and feel so thrilled to see you happy.

Was this love at first sight? One mother said, "Some people are fortunate enough to find deep and lasting love from the start. I believe that is true of Grace and Ed. It sounds corny, but these are two hearts in one. I'm delighted to say I'm a mom delirious with happiness for her daughter on this day. To Grace and Ed."

At a wedding where the bride's father had recently died, her mother toasted the groom: "Jared, I know you will take care of Frank's little girl." It was a way of almost speaking for the father, voicing what he might have said if he was there.

If the setting for the wedding is unique, you can also talk about that, as in this toast in which the father of the bride mentions the choice of a historic chapel: "Kumulani Chapel is a rustic little Hawaiian jewel over one hundred years old which Lorraine and I have passed many times. She loves it."

How have they influenced each other? You can say something like, "They've given each other courage to switch careers and enjoy more satisfying work," or, "She brings out his best qualities—and softens his edges. He encourages her to take creative chances."

GROOM'S TOAST TO THE BRIDE

Good sources for a toast include any creative work that touches upon the subject of true love, such as a movie or a poem. Check out some Shakespeare. Or how about the line from the film *As Good As It Gets*, spoken by Jack Nicholson: "You make me want to be a better man."

Think about why you are marrying this woman. What knocks you out about her? One groom toasted: "You have the same hopes and dreams I do. You make me laugh. You know me better and understand me better than anyone else in the world. I love you. To my sweetheart, Emily."

Another groom said, "I propose a toast to my beautiful bride, Janet, who makes me happy today and every day." Another: "To Lily, who is as good on the inside as she is beautiful on the outside." Or try, "I don't know how I got so fortunate, but I did win you. To my gorgeous bride."

BRIDE'S TOAST TO THE GROOM

A second-time bride toasted her new husband:

> *Making a commitment is like having a compass. You may not know where you're going—you may not even know where you are—but you always know which way is north. And you can figure the rest out from there.*
>
> *Jason, you are north on my compass. And while I don't know where I'm going, and sometimes don't even know where I am, I know we can figure the rest out from there.*

Think about how you feel about this man, as in, "You are my soulmate, my love, and my partner for life. Here's to you, Pete."

One bride toasted: "Like the song says, I'm in love with a wonderful guy. To Stan—you really *are* my hero."

Or how about, "I lost my heart to you on December twelfth one year ago. It will always be yours. To Jack."

TOASTS BY OTHERS

Is there a story in how they got together? Did they meet online, at the supermarket, while walking the dog, or in an elevator? All of these things might be fodder for a toast. One pair met through the Personals section of a magazine—the bride answered the groom's ad. A bridesmaid toasted:

> *First, I would like to congratulate Anna and Les on having the nerve to write and answer a personal ad. Second, I'd like to congratulate them on the energy they have put into their relationship. And they do have a lot of energy: bicycling, boating, nature walks, sailing, and country and western dancing. They genuinely do have fun together.*
>
> *I know that Anna and Les both love each other. Anna has told me that she has never been happier. Les has said that he is looking forward to spending his life with Anna. It has been a pleasure to watch them grow together—a vision I know most of you share. Please join me in a toast to Anna and Les. May your happiness at this moment be ever-lasting and may your love for each other abound forever.*

Some people actually put on a performance in tribute to the bride and groom. When her old college friend got married last year, a bridesmaid donned sunglasses, played the blues harmonica, and sang a little song she composed for the occasion, after this introduction:

Jen has always faced new and daunting challenges in her life with energy, enthusiasm, and courage. I'm delighted that she's found in Tim a partner who embraces life with the same energy and enthusiasm, and it's been a pleasure to get to know him.

Jen didn't really want to do the traditional "Something old, something new, something borrowed, and something blue" thing—but I wanted to make sure this evening that Jen at least got her blues.

REHEARSAL DINNER TOASTS

This dinner is held the night before the wedding and is hosted by the groom's family. It's an opportunity for the bride's clan and the groom's, who may be meeting for the first time, to mix and mingle, and it's usually an intimate and relaxed occasion. The father of the bridegroom (and perhaps the best man, as well) toasts the couple. Many of the suggestions for wedding toasts can be applied here. This is also a time to thank guests who have traveled a long way for making the trek.

One dad made the following moving tribute to his son and daughter-in-law to be (see the complete text in the Appendix). Speaking with enormous love, he said in part:

> . . . *I want to welcome you all to the "dinner the night before." We have people here tonight from a huge diversity of locations, including Oregon, California, Florida, Louisiana, Iowa, Virginia, Connecticut, Maryland, New York . . . Colombia and Chile. . . . I want to thank you all for coming to honor Cary and Bill. Some of the people here tonight have known Cary for a very long time and have met Bill on only a few occasions; others, the truly lucky ones in this room, have known them since they first began dating . . . almost six and a half years ago and have witnessed the growth of their relationship. I am blessed to be one of those people.*

The father went on to recall the first time he met the bride-to-be. He shared the memory of a Father's Day weekend he had expected to spend alone, due to the couple's work schedules. Then Cary called. Although Bill couldn't come along, she invited him to dinner with her at a restaurant. He said:

> *Once again it was a wonderful meal, and Cary presented me with a turquoise shell shaving set from her and Bill, along with a card. Moments later she reached in her purse and pulled out another card and said,*

"This is from me alone." The note read . . . "Dearest
Bob, Thank you so much for your loving and caring
ways. I feel as if the void that was left when my dad
died in 1993 is filled now that you are part of my life."

I was overwhelmed! I felt that now, not only did
I have an incredibly wonderful son, but a daughter
as well.

I raise this glass to toast the two of you—to the
wonderful, long, and happy marriage that I know you
will enjoy because of the three most impressive traits
you possess: The love that is so evident in your
relationship and which you so generously share with
your family and friends; Your accomplishments, which
are far too numerous to go into here; and last, your
passion for life, which defines who you are and which I
feel privileged to be a part of. I love you both so much.

The bride and groom can toast at the wedding reception, too, if
they wish. They can thank their parents, as well as out-of-town
guests.

One father of the bride toasted the couple, then acknowledged his wife with, "I want everyone to enjoy this wedding
because my wife has been working on it for twenty-five years for
her only daughter. Raise your glasses to her."

Anyone who wishes to do so can speak at a rehearsal dinner.
When one maid of honor was asked to organize the rehearsal
dinner toasts, she created a time capsule for the couple to open
on their fifth anniversary. At the dinner, any guest who wished to
speak could stand up, make a toast, and present a contribution

to the capsule. The toast focused on explaining the item and what it meant to the bride and groom.

The maid of honor launched the presentation by explaining the time capsule concept to the bride and groom, and then invited other guests to present their time capsule items. Her own contribution to the capsule was funny and personal.

"The bride and I have been best friends since age six," she remembers. "We often joked about how, when we married, we would be second only to our husbands for each other. So how could I be anything else than the center of attention? I had T-shirts printed for the bride and groom with a photo of myself on the front. I said, 'In five years, if you ever forget who was here first, you can wear these.' I explained to the room that I was involved in their relationship from the beginning. She would call me up and say, 'I'm dating this new guy. What do you think of him?' My opinion always mattered, and when she decided to marry him, I realized I'd no longer play the same role."

The groom's friends crooned their college fraternity song to the bride and placed a copy of the song in the capsule. One person snapped a picture of the couple and put it in the capsule, saying, "This will help you remember what you looked like on this night." And a family friend contributed a short slide presentation of the bride's parents' wedding, which he had attended thirty years before. His tribute to the bride and groom connected the two events, saying, "This is how *they* looked when they started. I wish you the same happiness."

Aside from being a good way to organize the toasts, the time capsule will provide precious memories. "There's so much going on at the rehearsal dinner; you're in a daze," the maid of honor said. "It's hard to remember everything that happens and what's said to you. This is a way to recapture it all."

She was able to contact the guests via e-mail beforehand, providing them with all of the information they needed, and the event went off without a hitch. "I was very nervous, but the idea worked. The theme was helpful to speakers, too, because it's hard to know where to begin when you have to give a toast. It's nice to be handed a 'job.' You also get to hear what other people did. It turned out to be such a memorable night and so much fun."

At another rehearsal dinner, a family friend used his talent for rhyme. This is part of his toast:

> *Here's to the groom and the bride,*
> *From those who're attending with pride.*
> *We're very impressed;*
> *We think you're the best,*
> *Although quite a few of us cried.*
>
> *Raise your glass to those getting married;*
> *For a while now your life has been harried,*
> *But soon you'll be wed*
> *And your single state shed—*
> *Then your lifestyle for sure will be varied.*
>
> *So, as you become man and wife,*
> *Then venture into your new life,*
> *We wish you fair weather*

> *In your life together,*
> *And never a moment of strife.*

Although the toast is general and could apply to any bride and groom, it was created by the speaker, not picked out of a book. Because the person obviously devoted time and effort to it, it is a gift to the couple. It could be followed up with personalization as in, "Bridget and John, I wish you many happy years together."

ENGAGEMENT PARTY TOASTS

The engagement party is usually hosted by the bride's family. Here the father of the bride-to-be can toast the couple, as in, "Here's to Sally and Bill. To love and happiness and all of your dreams together. I love you both."

Or how about, "Let's all drink to the happiness of Lila and Hank, to their love for each other, which is a pleasure to behold, and a life filled with joy ahead."

The groom may toast the bride at an engagement party, as in, "Amy, we've already shared our lives for three years. Now I—we—make a commitment to an unlimited future together. I want to spend it all with you. To Amy."

Anyone else who wants to join in can toast the couple and their parents. Just remember to keep it short. For example, an aunt toasted,

> *As I think about Pam and Roy walking down the*
> *aisle in a few months, I'm overwhelmed with*

memories of Pam's childhood—her love of books
and her passion for dance. She still fits those dance
lessons into her schedule. Roy, you've got a special
girl. She's got a special guy. Cherish each other.
Here's to you both.

Someone else toasted, "To Chris and Jen, We plan to dance with abandon at your wedding!" Couples love to hear that you're excited about their nuptials.

FOUR

ANNIVERSARIES

*E*ach wedding anniversary is a special moment for a couple, a time to reflect on their relationship and renew their commitment to each other. The celebration is ordinarily a private one, but if it's a milestone anniversary—the tenth or twentieth or fiftieth—the date may be marked by a festive dinner or party thrown by well-wishing friends and family. If you choose to say a few words on this occasion, remember that the point is to honor a marriage and tell the couple what they mean to you.

COMMENT ON THEIR RELATIONSHIP

If you know the marriage is a good one (and not all are), mention what you admire about it. On our last anniversary, a friend toasted my husband and me: "You've set an example of what two people who care about each other look like. Happy anniversary." A toast to another pair noted: "Not many couples still laugh at each other's jokes after all these years. You two do. You really like each other, and you inspire us all. To Karen and George."

This toast honored old school pals who were active in college theater: "It's hard to believe you're married twenty-two years because you still seem like two chorus kids about to break into the movies. You're as perfect for each other now as you were then. To Erica and Marvin. Happy anniversary."

Someone made this toast at a thirtieth anniversary celebration:

> *Joe and Madeline are a great match. She's the one*
> *out front, an extrovert; he's the quiet strength. They*
> *complement each other. Joe recently told me that*
> *they've been married all those years and have never*
> *spent a single night apart. They like it that way. We're*
> *thrilled to be here at their thirtieth anniversary*
> *celebration and we look forward to many more years*
> *of warm love at their house.*

On the other hand, if one or both of the spouses travels frequently, that can be turned around: "Harry is constantly boarding airplanes. But he's like a homing pigeon—always itching to get back to Gwen."

A shorter toast might go something like: "Here, here—to Phil and Ann, who have made a marriage which all of us admire." Simple, brief, but sweet.

These words toasted a sister and brother-in-law: "You're a couple who keeps evolving, in a relationship that is clearly informed by love and respect. Of the many achievements in your lives, this has to be the finest. Happy anniversary."

If it's a second (or third or fourth) marriage, you can acknowledge that, as in this toast to a childhood friend and her husband: "To Leila and Len. After the first time around, things get complicated. Yet you make it look effortless. Happy anniversary."

A tribute to a remarried couple, who are business partners as well as life partners, went:

Well, it took you guys a while to find each other, but some things are worth waiting for. You fit. It's dangerous to work together. Lots of couples get divorced. But you two just get stronger. In this case, love come late is the love that lasts. Here's to many more years of happiness.

REFER TO YOUR RELATIONSHIP WITH THE COUPLE

At a party, one woman reflected on how the pair stood by her when she needed them: "I won't ever forget how supportive you both are during tough times. When Bob's ninety-year-old mother lived with us for a year, we couldn't go out without her. Nobody would go out to dinner with us—except you. You're very special friends, and a wonderful pair. Happy anniversary."

Someone toasted friends: "Because you were married first, you've always been role models for our own marriage. You taught us how to fight and make up and how to survive a kitchen renovation without divorce. You're also the most fun on vacations. It's a pleasure to wish you a happy anniversary."

REMEMBER THEIR COURTSHIP OR THE WEDDING

There's nothing like nostalgia to stir the emotions—both yours and theirs. For a fortieth wedding anniversary party, a couple toasted the honorees: "Jim remembers your wedding well—he was best man, and someone spilled champagne all over his new tux. I remember your first anniversary, when we all went to a Broadway show to celebrate. It's great to be here, still celebrating. May you have many good years ahead. Happy fortieth."

When my cousin and her husband celebrated their fiftieth anniversary, they asked each guest to speak of a memory. My cousin had lived next door during my childhood. I said this:

> *I remember both of you going out together. I thought you were the most attractive pair on the planet. When you got married, remember how my mother and Aunt Rose showed up wearing the same long dress? Rose's was chartreuse; my mother's was cerise. They both*

*looked great, but we wondered how they could have
chosen the same style while living (and shopping)
hundreds of miles apart.*

*You were a storybook bride and groom and your
wedding was definitely the social event of my
childhood. Everyone looked so happy. I've always
remembered. You have my love and admiration.*

If you can't or don't want to talk about the couple's wedding day, use your toast to reminisce about that other important day in their lives—the day they first met. Did they strike up a conversation on the red-eye from L.A. or on a bus? I know of someone who met his wife in a chiropractor's waiting room. This might become a funny lead-in to a toast. One friend repeated what he'd been told, saying, "Laura regaled me with her early impression of Hank. 'He had a Picasso print on the wall and Mozart on the stereo. I thought he was so intellectual.'"

You can also relate how you met them, if it's a good story like this one:

*We were in the process of taking pictures on a
parapet in the Dordogne, squeezed into this narrow
space, and Pete, then a stranger, with his well-known
patience, decided it had gone far enough. He offered
to take the photos for us. We started to talk with him
and Melinda, and three hours later we all agreed to
meet again the next day. We've arranged to meet every
year since.*

The storytellers then passed around copies of a "book" they had made at a copier store, featuring photos from past vacations with the anniversary couple.

MARVEL AT MILESTONES

A twenty-fifth or fiftieth anniversary is an accomplishment these days. However, a first or tenth or indeed any subsequent number ending in five (15, 25, 35, etc.) is also a reason to cheer. Mention how the occasion makes you feel, as in, "In the era of disposable relationships, I feel awed to see your marriage so fresh and happy after all these years."

Talk about a long marriage as an achievement. Someone toasted a couple wed twenty-five years: "It's a challenge to live with someone that long and keep your marriage interesting. Yet you always keep each other guessing. And, not incidentally, you've raised two wonderful kids in difficult times. Be proud and happy. We love you."

Or try a quote: "Benjamin Disraeli said it destroys your nerves to be amiable every day to the same human being. But somehow you two have stayed calm and content for thirty-five years. We need to know your secrets. To Greta and Dave."

How about: "Ginger Rogers said, 'When two people love each other, they don't look at each other, they look in the same direction.' June and Dan have looked in the same direction together for twenty-five years."

For a short take on the same idea, consider, "To a marriage for always."

Of course, humor isn't off-limits in an anniversary toast, either. "And they said it wouldn't last" is a great way to start a toast for a thirtieth anniversary, or any long marriage. Everyone will giggle.

MENTION THEIR PLANS

People often celebrate their anniversary with a special trip. Are they sailing to England on the *QEII* or spending a week cruising through the Norwegian fjords? Use the information, as in, "As you watch the midnight sun, we'll be thinking of you. To Susan and Jim. Happy anniversary." (If he bought her a new diamond wedding band, it doesn't hurt to mention that, too!)

At a sixty-second anniversary dinner, a niece toasted a couple about to move from an apartment to a senior residence. She said:

> *To Aunt Nina and Uncle Harry. Happy anniversary. Think of how pleasant life is going to be at Four Oaks. Everything's taken care of for you—and oh, those terrific meals. You'll be there before you know it. And remember we're here to help.*

For younger couples, you can refer to their new baby or new house (or even a new car), as in, "Happy anniversary, Jan and Simon. You've already started celebrating with your new van. Here's to more good things in the year ahead."

TOASTING YOUR SPOUSE

An anniversary is, in the end, a private and personal ritual for two people. It's a transition when you tend to take stock of your relationship. You can refer to your commitment to each other, how you've changed, and the ups and downs you've shared, as in, "To Deborah: We're still here—twelve years and counting. I love you more than ever." Or, "Through thick and thin we've stayed steady." Or, "We've rolled with the punches to grow stronger than ever. Happy anniversary, my love."

On our last anniversary, my husband toasted me: "You're my love, my inspiration, and my best friend. I love you more than words can say. Happy anniversary, hon."

A sampling of some other husband-wife toasts:

"Some of us get lucky. I did. I got you. Happy anniversary, sweetheart."

"When I first met you, you took my breath away. After sixteen years, you still do. Happy anniversary."

"Each year, as you grow older and wiser, you become more beautiful. I can hardly wait until you are eighty. Happy anniversary."

"You're the only man for me. Always were, always will be. To Craig."

"You're not only great to cuddle up with at night, you're my sweetheart and dearest pal. Happy anniversary."

"I'm a happy man. I've been blessed with twenty years with the sexiest, wittiest, most loyal lady I know. To the only woman I've ever loved."

If the two of you are celebrating privately, by all means use all those silly endearing names you have for each other (like "sweetie pie"). I call my own husband everything from "honey bunny" to "kookaburra bird." Don't ask me why. It's my language of love. Psychologists say such names are a sign of affection for each other.

TOASTING RELATIONSHIPS WITH "SIGNIFICANT OTHERS"

Sometimes you're celebrating the anniversary of a relationship that doesn't involve marriage. An estimated one to two million people in the United States live together in long-term committed relationships, according to *American Demographics* magazine. You can generally use the same techniques mentioned for married couples (except, of course, for memories of the wedding).

To close friends of mine, together for fifteen years, I recently toasted:

> *I just realized that you two are totally different. Bill*
> *is the eternal optimist; Joan is the cynic. Yet you*
> *never try to change each other. You're completely*
> *accepting. No wonder you're so happy together.*
> *Here's to the good years ahead.*

You can also refer to their arrangement, as in, "You have been together a lot longer than most married couples I know. The love you so clearly feel for each other makes all of us glow. We wish you many more years of happiness."

FIVE

BIRTHDAYS

*Y*our birthday is the one day of the year when you can be the center of attention and feel truly special. Since approximately five million Americans celebrate their birthdays every week, according to Hallmark, there's a good chance you'll know one of them! Whether the setting is a living room or a restaurant, birthday parties are great opportunities to make toasts and tributes and show people how much they mean to you. If you're invited to a birthday celebration, it's probably because you know the person (and at least some of the other guests) very well. You can draw upon insights and history to say, "I care about you," and reinforce the bonds you share.

EXPRESS YOURSELF

It's okay to get sentimental and nostalgic and tell people you love them. One recipient of a heartwarming toast was a stepmother who had worked hard to build caring relationships with her husband's family, baby-sitting for the grandchildren and befriending her new stepdaughters. One of the stepdaughters told this woman how much she meant to the family with a simple but meaningful birthday toast: "To Jenny. Our lives are richer because of you. Happy birthday."

At another party, someone toasted a best pal *and* the friendship: "You're true to yourself and never afraid to say the wrong thing. You're generous—and you love the same crazy movies I do. I'm so lucky to have you as a friend and I know it. Happy birthday."

You don't need to be sentimental, though, if that's not your style. Humor can be just as charming. At one twenty-fifth birthday, a young woman played a song on her guitar that she'd written for a friend. Part of it went:

> *Twenty-five's a mighty nice number:*
> *It's one-fourth of a century,*
> *It's the number of cents in a quarter,*
> *And a little bit older than me.*

COMMENT ON WHAT'S GOING ON
IN THE PERSON'S LIFE

It's a way to personalize your words. Did a friend bag an important new piece of business? Raise a glass and say something like, "Joe, I have the feeling this is the beginning of a banner year for you. You've a right to feel proud of yourself. Happy birthday."

A niece offered this toast to a beloved uncle who was about to move from Washington, D.C., to New York City: "To Uncle Randy. Have a happy birthday—and give our regards to Broadway!"

If the honoree is a young person, you can refer to school, or starting a new job, or other activities or interests, as in, "To the busiest freshman at the University of Texas. I wish you the happiest of birthdays." Or, "Mary, you've got a lot to look forward to. Here's to interesting challenges and success at Boyd & Co. Happy birthday."

A group of friends recited this toast to someone who was recovering from major surgery:

> *We toast you, our cherished friend,*
> *We're so thrilled you're on the mend;*
> *May good times prevail, so you can party,*
> *And continue to feel hale and hearty!*
> *Happy birthday!*

As with this hospital patient, you don't have to shy away from difficult issues when giving a toast; in fact, your toast will seem more sincere if you address important happenings in the person's life, even if they're not happy events. A wife whose husband had been seriously ill toasted him like this: "This is a year of renewal for you. I know life isn't perfect yet, but by next year, you're going to be a tiger. Happy birthday, love."

Another thing to remember is that you don't need a crowd to make a toast; sometimes the sweetest toasts can happen between only two people. Once I took a friend who had just written her first novel out to lunch for her birthday and said: "Here's to finding a publisher fast! Happy birthday."

You don't have to focus on past accomplishments, either. Try toasting with a list of what you know the person would like to accomplish in the year ahead, as in, "Barbara, this is your year for learning how to get online, joining a health club, and finally cutting your hair. Happy birthday."

CONSIDER HOW THE PERSON FEELS ABOUT THE BIRTHDAY

Birthdays signify different things to different people. Ask yourself, What does this day mean to the person? and then craft your toast accordingly. Because children are excited to be a year older, you can elicit a giggle with something like, "Jimmy, it's hard to believe how big you're getting. You're actually seven! Happy birthday." To a teenager you can try, "Bobby, sixteen is a milestone year. You'll get your driver's license soon, and you're already planning for college. What a year! Happy birthday."

On the other hand, hitting forty—or fifty or sixty, for that matter—can be traumatic, so skip the "How wonderful, it's your birthday" comments. For a friend turning fifty, I made this tribute: "Elaine, the fifties are splendid years, as you're going to find out—full of discovery, freedom, and satisfaction for anyone who's up for it. I wish you all this and more. Happy birthday."

To someone turning forty, a family member said, "I just read that once they pass forty, more and more people are satisfied with their lives. Think of all the happiness ahead! Here's to you, Justin."

In a similar vein, a childhood friend of a woman turning sixty made this tribute: "Meg, when you get past the shock, the question, How can this be happening to me? you realize that you're the same as you were at fifty-nine—only better. Since you're the best, and always have been, you don't have to change a thing. I wish you blessings ahead. Happy birthday, dear friend."

Think about marital status, too. A married thirty-year-old woman may feel very different from a single one who feels the pressure of time passing. Loving support is appropriate for the latter, as in, "Here's to possibilities. Happy birthday."

IDENTIFY PERSONAL TRAITS

For someone's forty-fourth birthday, a friend toasted: "Allison is my idol. Who else has the moxie to launch a new career at this age and make it look easy? She lives life at full throttle and never looks back. To Allison—a fantastic friend. Happy birthday."

Another pal added: "You have given me so many gifts. You've taught me so much about style. You always have a kind word. You support anything I want to do, and you're always there for me. I'm so happy to have you in my life."

Is the honoree an elderly person who's still young at heart? Say so. A granddaughter made this tribute for her ninety-year-old grandmother, who resided at an assisted living facility:

I'm pretty lucky I've got a grandmother who's never lost her spark and sense of fun. She's still ready to go for a ride or shopping or to lunch at a moment's notice. And she dresses like a fashion plate, too. Grandma, I'm glad I've got your genes. I'm thrilled to be here with you celebrating your ninetieth. I love you.

Another toaster identified her daughter's strongest character traits in this birthday tribute:

From the day Susan came into this world, curiosity was her mantle; when she became ambulatory, she ran and seldom walked. I confess that both then and now I've had a hard time keeping up with her, literally and figuratively.

When her father left us, she became the embodiment of his spirit of adventure and his sense of honesty and justice.

To my daughter, my friend, who is constantly a challenge and catalyst for growth—happy birthday.

REACH BACK FOR MEMORIES

A friend at a birthday dinner reminisced: "I'm like the little sister he never had—he loves to tease me! I remember the time we were in California, and he chased me through the park with a rolled newspaper. I was laughing so hard because I had smacked him and he was trying to get back at me. Here was this dignified executive chasing me."

One woman scoured her mother's address book on the occasion of her eightieth birthday. She asked everyone listed to fill in a "memories card," describing their connection with her mom, a prolific letter writer. One of the responses, which were read aloud at the party, went like this: "I was sitting on a bench waiting for a bus and this nice woman introduced herself to me. That conversation led to a friendship I've always cherished, and we've been corresponding for twenty-five years." These memories were collected in a book, which was then presented to the mother.

One way to inspire your own ideas is to glance through your family photo album. Then you can say to your sister or cousin something like, "I just came across a snapshot of both of us pregnant. We looked like tubs, but we had so many laughs. It was a long time ago, but you're still my best buddy. Happy birthday."

At a colleague's birthday celebration, someone recalled in verse:

I remember a trip to Houston
When you traveled by plane,
And carried barbecue back home;
You drove the stewardess insane.

The ice chest was in the compartment above.
"What's this?" The stewardess said as she gave it
*   a shove.*

> *When the sauce, red like blood, began to drip ever*
> *so slow,*
> *You said, "It's my spare heart. I carry it wherever*
> *I go."*

She followed this poem with a few eloquent remarks about the fun she was having at the party. This is always a good addition to a toast, no matter what the occasion, because it thrills people to hear that guests are having a good time.

You can also connect a memory to the person's current occupation. A sister told her brother, "Remember when you caught your foot in your bike and we ran to the emergency room to get you stitches? Who knew you'd wind up a paramedic. Well, now you are—and a good one, too. We're proud of you. Many happy returns."

On her son's twenty-eighth birthday, a mother remembered:

> *The other day, Eddie called and said, "What are you*
> *doing, Mom? Would you like to have lunch with me?"*
> *It was the best gift anyone ever gave me. The*
> *sweetness of it—and of him. That's just one of the*
> *reasons I love you, Eddie. Happy birthday.*

Working in a person's hobby or interest can help personalize your words, too. A son toasted his mother: "We all know about Mom's exploits as a weekend gardener, but Mom, your garden is not the only thing that has grown more lovely over time. Happy sixtieth, Mom."

PHILOSOPHIZE ON AGING

As people get older, they tend to look at the past and at the future on their birthdays. You can mention goals ahead, such as retirement, or you can express pride in the person's past accomplishments. This toast honored a friend and colleague making midlife career changes: "Some people hit fifty-five and feel it's the beginning of the end. For Liz, it's a new beginning—of teaching the literature she loves, and patiently awaiting what else develops. To Liz! Happy birthday." It's a wonderful gift when you can make another person feel understood.

This toast was made to an eighty-year-old:

> *I read somewhere that old age is fifteen years older*
> *than you are. In your case, Ethel, it may be twenty*
> *years. Once thing is certain, it sure isn't now. I, for*
> *one, can't keep up with you. Here's to a very happy*
> *birthday and a healthy year ahead. With your new*
> *pacemaker, I'm sure it will be.*

Or how about using this quote: "Katherine Hepburn said, 'I have no romantic feelings about age. Either you are interesting at any age or you are not.' Janine, you've always been interesting—not to mention dynamic. Good luck on the new business, and have a very happy birthday."

Someone said to a fifty-eight-year-old: "Time passes and you're one year older—but you're never old. Happy birthday,

Greg." For the right person, "You're a classic!" might fit as a one-liner.

TRY HUMOR

My sons made this toast to me on a recent birthday: "Because the only thing harder than being a mother is being *our* mother, we, of course, wish you the mother of all great birthdays. We love you, Mom."

If you call any woman a "goddess" after fifty, she'll laugh— and love you for it. At one surprise birthday party (hosted by the honoree's husband), guests arrived at a Manhattan pier and boarded a ship, which then cruised around New York Harbor for the evening. A friend wrote and delivered this poetic tribute:

> *Betty dear,*
> *This is a treat,*
> *Meeting all your friends*
> *On 43rd Street.*
>
> *All birthdays are nice,*
> *But this one is great;*
> *That's why we're here—*
> *We wouldn't miss this date.*
>
> *Off on a cruise,*
> *To heaven knows where;*

The weather's great—
And Harold paid the fare!

Some things may change
As the years go by:
Our clothes don't fit,
And we're not so spry.

We can't remember
What pills we took,
Or what on earth
We did with that book.

But you don't have wrinkles,
And you look like a lass;
As a person of forty
You could certainly pass.

So now, Miss E——,
We lift our glass
To wish good cheer
To a lady of class.

But there's one more thing,
Which you must now face:
You can no longer accuse your spouse
Of never taking you anyplace!

SIX

HOLIDAYS AND FAMILY

CELEBRATIONS

$\mathcal{T}$hanksgiving, Christmas, and other occasions are a chance for families to get together. On these days, we can reconnect with who we are, who we were, and where we came from. Holidays are also a good excuse for the span of generations to mingle, play catch-up, and renew emotional ties (without cell phones!).

A holiday toast can help everyone relax and reaffirm bonds of kinship. Some families even have their own time-honored favorites that have been handed down through the years.

Whether toasts have already been a tradition in your family or you want to begin the ritual this year, consider the ideas that follow. They will work for a "family" which consists of blood relatives or dear friends.

TAKE TURNS AROUND THE TABLE

You can be the person who says a few words or you can take the lead and encourage everyone else to toast. This allows even the youngest guests to participate and feel included. It is also a great way to welcome in-laws, new friends, or others.

COMMENT ON FAMILY NEWS

One host toasted his architect cousin, who had recently won a professional award, with, "We know Pete as the guy we all turn to when there's a crisis in the family or when we need sage advice. And he always knows what to do, always has answers for us. In the outside world, he plays another role, and it's particularly gratifying to see him recognized by the Landmarks Society as winner of their annual award. To Pete. We're awfully proud of you."

You can also recognize the little events which aren't so little to the person involved. How about, "Here's to Bobby for making the soccer team. Go get 'em, champ!"

If someone has been ill, try "We all understand this year that life is a gift. To good health for all of us." A college student toasted a recuperating relative: "Uncle Sam, you lost a lot of weight in the hospital, but your heart is still big. Here's to you."

RECALL A FAMILY MEMORY

Talk about a wedding when uncle Mo got tipsy and danced the jitterbug. Reminisce about a reunion or family vacation, then toast what good sports you all are in volleyball (a family trait). Close with, "To the Joneses and the Smiths." Remembering the fun you've had together helps you feel close.

SHOW-AND-TELL

Pull out your photo album, allowing everyone to ooh and ah at family snapshots. Then you can toast: "Here's to more good times together!"

It doesn't have to be complicated, either. A traditional toast for one family is, "Here's to us. There's none better!"

TOAST THE HOST OR HOSTESS

One nonprofit executive I know loves to entertain. She is a consummate hostess, and you're not invited to her house unless she does all the cooking herself. Her husband regularly toasts her with something like, "To my sweetheart. I've been watching you at a distance, slaving for the last week. Everybody's sitting around the table enjoying the food, but they don't know what love went into its preparation."

She admits, "I adore it when he toasts me on the holidays when I've been cooking up a storm. Now I'm spoiled. If he doesn't toast me, I think I did something wrong."

It's also appreciated when guests thank the host or hostess with a toast, as in, "Julia, I don't know how you do it. Most people blanch at feeding *six* people. You entertain twenty of us and make it look easy. Thanks for a wonderful time."

THANKSGIVING TOASTS

For me, Thanksgiving is the ultimate family event, a time for aunts, uncles, cousins, grandparents, and everyone else to spend a day together. Often friends also inject a fresh perspective to the festivities. At our house, we drink a little wine and eat without reservation; the result is laughter, silliness, and a certain honesty about ourselves. Such community is so rare these days that it's worth commemorating.

For your toast, you can give thanks for the good in your lives. Hold up your glass and list all the things your family is grateful for this year, as in, "How lucky we are that Gary is doing well at the University of Illinois, Lisa has a great new job at Bank of America, and Steven and Andrea have moved into their new apartment." Continue around the table, covering everyone. It's an opportunity to celebrate the younger generation and there's always something positive you can say. Then close with, "Here's to good health and happiness for us all." Because my son's birthday is November 30 and my niece's is November 17, I always present a joint cake and candles on Thanksgiving—and we toast them both.

A friend of mine in California uses this Spanish toast on such occasions: *"Salud, amor, y pesetas, y el tiempo para gustarlos,"* which means "Health, love, and money, and the time to enjoy it."

CHRISTMAS TOASTS

Some people say the holidays are disappointing because they never live up to expectations. Yet they can also fill us with hope, and become a nurturing gift to the children in the family. Think about Christmases past and reminisce. Memories warm us. Depending on whether you regard Christmas as strictly social or as a deeply religious occasion, you can toast to peace on earth, reflect on the birth of Christ, or focus family strengths. The warmth and good feelings can last for days afterward.

You can also add a little humor with something like, "It's said that you gain seven or more pounds between Christmas and New Year's. Well today's sumptuous dinner will certainly account for a big chunk of it. Here's to our host and hostess."

Someone commented on the Christmas dinner fare with this toast: "I just read that we raise 210,000 geese a year in the United States, most of them in North Dakota, of all places. Patty cooked our goose today—and a fine one it is. Don't know where it's from, but it looks good. To Patty, our chef."

NEW YEAR'S TOASTS

Of course you're going to toast the New Year. Whether you celebrate at home or out at a party, you can mention New Year's resolutions, starting with your own, as in, "Here's to a great (year). Can't speak for you, but I hereby resolve to flatten my tummy and take a pottery class."

If you live in a cold climate, you might try something like, "Hang on! Spring is only three months away. I can almost smell the lilacs. Happy New Year." Or, "May love nourish us all through the rest of the winter. To us."

Consider what's ahead for the people you are with. Is someone floundering personally or professionally? You might toast, "May you find all you're looking for in the New Year," or, "The New Year is a clean slate. To exciting opportunities in (year.)"

Other possibilities:

"We value your friendship more and more. Here's to more good times in (year)."

"May next year bloom with all good things. To the best New Year."

"To peace and prosperity at your house and ours in (year)."

"To the happily unexpected in (year)."

EASTER TOASTS

Celebrating the Resurrection of Jesus, Easter is a time for gatherings, churchgoing, and reinforcing ties. A toast is something you can do to help everyone feel the power and warmth of family. You can also refer to Easter bunnies, comment on everyone's bonnets, or if you're in a spiritual mood, say something like, "Easter eggs are actually a symbol of renewal. Here's to a season of new beginnings for all of us."

MOTHER'S DAY TOASTS

Tell your mother that she's special and has done a good job—that's what she wants to hear on Mother's Day. Make her happy.

Reflect on what she means to you. Raise your glass and toast her with something like, "How did I get so lucky to have you as a mom? I love you. To Mom." Or, "To Mother. You deserve a lot more than just a day of recognition. You're the best!" Or, "Mom, you're quite a woman. Here's to you on Mother's Day."

Or, "You're the star of our show. You keep the whole family on track. To Mom. We love you dearly." Or, "To Mother. Thank you for all you do."

Don't forget your mother-in-law. Try "To Helen. Thanks for your love and support all year long. We love you."

FATHER'S DAY TOASTS

Think of the role your dad has played in your life, and let him know that you appreciate him. Your toast might say something like, "You never missed my Little League games," or, "You were always a troublemaker and you taught me to stand up for my convictions," or, "Dad, you taught me the art of persistence. You're a special man. Here's to you."

Or refer to his hobby or interest as in, "To the best bridge player (or fisherman) in the neighborhood. Happy Father's Day." Or, "Let's raise our glasses to Dad. Good luck in the golf tournament. We're all rooting for you. Love you a lot."

TOASTS FOR THE BIRTH
OF A BABY

This is a joyous event. Sound like it. Toast the baby, as in:

"To the delicious Isabel, the new family jewel."

Or, "To Christopher—our future."

Or, "Here's to Amy. You're a honey in every way."

Or toast the parents, as in, "To Jane and Paul. You won't lack for baby-sitters. We're all fighting over Daniel already."

Since new parents tend to feel insecure, it's particularly nice to reassure them with: "To Patsy and Steve. What great parents you're going to be!" They'll love you forever for that one.

If the pregnancy was difficult or long-awaited, you can speak to that, too. One couple tried unsuccessfully to have children for years, finally accepting that they would not. Then the wife, to her own surprise, became pregnant—with twins. When the babies were born, a friend toasted, "To two beautiful miracles and their joyful parents. To Hannah and Seth."

In another case where a couple overcame infertility problems, someone toasted the baby: "To Michael—you were a long time arriving, but worth the wait."

A public relations manager had her first baby two months after her beloved grandmother died. Her cousin toasted, "Baby Caroline is part of the circle of life—and of love. To Caroline's adoring parents, Jeri and Scott, and to a new generation."

You can allude to the family, too, especially in an adoption, with, "Billy is a lucky baby. He's joining a wonderful family."

GRADUATION TOASTS

Remember that this is a landmark event in a young person's life. Think about the accomplishment, discipline, and responsibility involved. Was he or she a top student, on the debating team, or involved in volunteer activities? Mention it.

You can also talk about what's next—job, college, military, graduate school. To a high school graduate, someone toasted, "Mike, in Sanskrit, *veda* means knowledge. And that's what you're about to get a lot of in the next four years at UCLA. Here's to success ahead—and fun. We're very proud of you." *Any* graduate wants to hear those last five words.

To someone who has made career plans, try something like, "Linda, you're going to be a great veterinarian (or teacher or filmmaker). Here's to you." Or, "Tom, here's to a triumph in law school. You've got what it takes." For any kind of graduate school, you can refer to the hard work involved, or the investment in money and time, and how it will pay off in the long run.

If the person barely graduates, the toast may be trickier. What can you say to someone who was not a star? How about, "To Tom. Here's to four years of discovery ahead." Or, "To Jane. Figure out what it takes to make you happy and go for it." Or, "May you find your dream and pursue it." Or, "Bob, you're a work in progress, becoming who you are. You make us proud."

SEVEN

ROASTS

$\mathcal{A}$ roast is an event that recognizes someone using humor and satire. The honoree, who has agreed in advance to subject himself or herself to this abuse, is raked over the coals—but never with malice. The underlying emotions are always affection and admiration.

Funny jokes and embarrassing stories about the person are the highlights of roasts, which are suitable for such occasions as birthdays, bachelor and bachelorette parties, and retirements. To skewer someone skillfully, however, you must know your target and audience well. The audience must know you, too—in order to understand what you're saying and realize that the remarks are meant to be humorous, not wounding.

If you are asked to participate in a roast, plan to speak for three to five minutes maximum. You're not the only person who will be talking. Here are some techniques to help you come up with barbed but affectionate remarks for a roast.

EXAGGERATE AND DISTORT

Exaggeration is the stuff of roasts. You begin with something true about the person (such as her addiction to french fries or candy) and take off from there, as in, "We all know about Joan and her cache of chocolate-covered raisins in the drawer."

Says one man who's in demand to participate in roasts because he's so good at them, "It brings down the house to lampoon the most important person in the room about traits others may recognize but would never mention, such as his pomposity. Everyone has seen these qualities, but they like him anyway. You can say things that are close to the truth. The key is to be honest about the person and loving. It's 'All this is true, but we're not all perfect and wonderful, and we love you anyway.'"

Ironically, your barbs actually help cast the honoree in a good light because others see that he's a good sport and approachable. This brings a warm spirit to the room.

SLANT TO THE AUDIENCE

In the case of a job-related roast, you'll naturally base your remarks on what the audience is likely to know and understand about the person, such as his or her work history, education, accomplishments, and opinions about the business or profession.

Let's say the honoree is someone who travels a lot. One roaster quipped, "I'm going to talk fast because Bob leaves at nine P.M. for Fiji." That's funny to people who know he virtually lives on airplanes. Is someone famous for worrying so much about missing a flight that he gets to the airport hours earlier than necessary? You might ride him with, "John's got to go to the airport tonight. He leaves for Chicago tomorrow at noon." Such comments, especially when said slowly and with a straight face, will be uproariously funny to anyone who knows John's foibles.

MINE A VARIETY OF SOURCES

You can lampoon someone whether or not you're a born comedian. There's material in everything: appearance (a bald head or skinny legs); clothing (loud ties); past mistakes (stock losses); eating habits ("Al's idea of gourmet food is tacos"); or occupation ("Like all lawyers, Bob specializes in billings"). You can even recall embarrassing moments in the person's career.

Family members can be dragged in, too, as when one "roaster" attributed all of the honoree's successes to his wife. And when one bride was roasted all night at her bachelorette party, not one ex-boyfriend was left out of the discourse, from "Jimmy the Jerk" to "Cheapo Charley."

LIST THE PERSON'S FAULTS

Do this gently! "You do want to be a little on edge, but not sarcastic," advises one veteran roaster. Is the honoree someone who's known for being disorganized? Try stating the opposite for humorous effect—compliment him on his detail skills.

With a straight face, try: "How do we admire you? Let us count the ways. We admire you for your even temper (to someone who often blows his cool) . . . your taste in suits (for someone who wears only jeans) . . . your punctuality (for someone always late) . . . your neatness (for someone whose desk is always a disaster area) . . . for your spontaneity and flexibility (for someone whose desk is always spotless with not a paper in sight)."

There is a point where you draw the line and express affection for the person. And then you hit him one more time.

KNOW YOUR TARGET

At a retirement party for a female department head, someone did a takeoff on "The 2,000-Year-Old Man." She was the 2,000-year-old woman, who had dated people in history. She was a good sport, laughing along with everyone else. The speaker knew she would take his teasing in good humor. But you must be certain to gauge the honoree's reactions realistically. You don't want to hurt or anger anyone.

You need a close connection to the person because he has to know where you're coming from in order to accept the insults. If you have a history together, he knows that if the tables were turned you wouldn't mind being roasted yourself.

BEWARE OF POOR TASTE

Some roasts are scathing, and that's okay as long as you know your target and your audience. You don't want to cross the line. Keep sex, bathroom humor, or other offensive material out of it.

You're not here to cause harm and you don't want to touch on sensitive issues. Remember, you *are* honoring someone!

BE SELF-DEPRECATING

Roasts are one occasion when it's appropriate to put yourself down. If you dish it out, you have to be able to take it. One roaster who's only five foot seven often says, "I just got back from basketball practice," which gets people laughing. He's also not above putting on a silly costume to make people smile.

REBUTTAL

The honoree always has the last word at the mike, replying to all the barbs received. If that's you, make notes of the quips, then take one of the comments about you and top it yourself, with something like, "My wife *likes* my skinny legs, and they're actually handy in a pinch. When I run out of socks, I borrow hers."

You can also make a list of the roasters, and retort by lampooning *them*, using some of the techniques previously mentioned. One man was the butt of a surprise fortieth birthday party thrown by colleagues. He was roasted with songs and a slide show of his life. At the end, he went around the room making a quip about each person. He is good at this, but even if you're not, relax. The audience consists of people who are disposed to laugh; it's the context and the spirit of the occasion. Open your mouth and chances are they'll already be giggling.

business and

professional occasions

EIGHT

AWARDS AND HONORS

$\mathcal{E}$very year, the Fund for the City of New York presents awards to unsung heroes of public service. Honorees range from a teacher who runs a successful gym program in an underresourced Brooklyn school to a planner who created a map of the city's infrastructure. Throughout the country, it's common for chambers of commerce, businesses, universities, and other organizations to pay tribute to noteworthy people with awards and honors. At these ceremonies, someone will often stand up and offer a testimonial saluting the honoree; it helps to have a method to engage the audience and say something of substance. Expect to speak for up to three or four minutes.

ASK YOURSELF WHY
THIS HONOREE IS SPECIAL

Will the person's achievements save lives, bring jobs or resources to the community, or speed the transfer of information? Explain how he accomplished what he did and why it is important. For example, if a company has won an award for innovation, you can explore what's daring about its policies or direction and how the company challenges the status quo.

At a testimonial dinner, explain why the person is being honored, as in, "We're here to salute Bob's groundbreaking contributions to film production," or, "For the last decade, Jim has singlehandedly boosted awareness of environmental issues." Or, "It's a pleasure to recognize John's extraordinary service to United Way. We're here to thank him."

Ask, too, What can *I* bring to the event? Do I feel strongly about the cause or issues involved? Great speeches spring from genuine involvement and passion.

What positive feelings can you express? A state pharmacists society offers a "Friend of the Pharmacy Award" to a physician who has promoted better patient care by improving doctor-pharmacist communication. In this case, illustrate the impact of such relationships with a personal anecdote. Expressions of your admiration, respect, or even affection (if you know the honoree well) can profoundly touch the audience.

DESCRIBE THE AWARD
AND WHAT IT SIGNIFIES

You might say, "The Year 2002 Fashion First Award is a public way to recognize outstanding promotion of the footwear industry." Or, "The Louis B. Johnson Prize honors an educator who has demonstrated lifelong commitment to the nation's schools." Or, "This award recognizes companies that have spearheaded regional growth." Or, "Winners of this award change lives. They do it literally and they do it figuratively, by giving the elderly dignity and the means to live a decent quality of life."

If you were saluting winners of the public service award mentioned at the beginning of this chapter, you might say, "This award honors service, compassion, and commitment to the city beyond the call of duty. The winners have responded to public needs by cutting red tape and developing more effective delivery of services." You could also mention the nature of the award itself. In this instance, it's a check for $7,500.

GET SPECIFIC

Eyes glaze over at generalities, but details hold audience attention. Illustrate the winner's impact or achievement, as in, "We're here tonight to honor John Smith, a man who is truly a wizard. In five years he's transformed a small company into an industry powerhouse. When other businesses were hemorrhaging employees, he attracted the best talents and kept them."

When the president of a trade association presented a plaque to an attorney, he said:

*For the last decade, Gary A. Small has been our
champion. Representing us before the FTC and
other federal agencies, he has gotten regulations
favorable to the industry. He helped persuade
Congress to pass the legislation we need to do
business in today's global economy. One of our
biggest challenges is dealing with the bureaucracy.
And nobody does it better or faster than Gary. We
wouldn't be where we are without your advice and
guidance, Gary. To show our appreciation for your
efforts on behalf of our industry since 1991, with
great pride I present this plaque.*

(Incidentally, when presenting a trophy or a scroll, do pay attention to the little things. In one instance, the honoree's name
was misspelled, causing unnecessary embarrassment for all con-
cerned. The plaque had to be redone.)

If the sponsoring organization is a charity or cause, in most
cases the honoree will be someone who has a genuine concern
for it. Describe that connection. For example, a tribute to Arnold
Schwarzenegger, recipient of the Simon Wiesenthal Center's 1997
National Leadership Award, honored the actor's support of the
Center and its Museum of Tolerance (see the Appendix for the
full text). The tribute said in part:

*[Arnold] has been a major contributor and fund-
raiser. . . . Years ago Arnold got involved in the
Center, and was among the first of the Hollywood
stars to do so. He was well ahead of his time and*

certainly has done this without a great deal of recognition. He has raised awareness in the non-Jewish community and most importantly has made a commitment to ensure that this dedication of principles will continue not only though the next generation but for generations to come.

The executive director of a nonprofit explains, "I think the honoree really has to have a personal connection because people feel it when they're in a room. Warmth is the big thing. When you're running a charity you always want people to feel wonderful when they leave so that when they get the invitation the next year, they'll remember, 'I had such a nice time. It was so moving, and it was over at nine o'clock. Yes, I want to go.'"

If the person you are praising is a stranger to you, as in the case of a celebrity honoree, dig for the background information you need. Talk to those who *do* know him or her, and ask them to suggest additional sources. Read his biography, if there is one and check newspaper or magazine articles about him.

If there have been other well-known winners, mention a few to indicate the fine company the honoree has joined, as in, "Past winners of the Innovation Awards include several of the boldest names in the industry, such as Dell and Microsoft."

TALK ABOUT THE HONOREE'S SPECIAL QUALITIES

A good tribute lets the audience know what the honoree is all about. Search for lively anecdotes or quotations that illustrate character and personality; these things add signature power to your message. At a professional organization's awards ceremony, a speaker remembered her first contact with the honoree. She had called to ask the person to appear on a panel for the organization. Instead of trying to wriggle out of a commitment, the honoree simply said, "It's a good cause. Yes." In five words, the quote spoke volumes about the person.

At a marketing awards dinner, the presenter opened with, "Dag Hammarskjöld once said, 'Life only demands from you the strengths you possess. Only one feat is possible—not to have run away.' On that basis, James Post is the most fearless guy around. He's a maverick who stands up for his principles and faces up to his mistakes. He knows when to let go. If something doesn't work, he finds alternatives that do succeed."

But you can also say something as simple as, "George is a true Southern gentleman. He speaks softly. He's also a spectacular fund-raiser." Or "George is a 'take charge' guy. He doesn't wait to react to change; he anticipates it, and acts accordingly."

EXPLORE THE PERSON'S BACKGROUND

The Schwarzenegger tribute was essentially a résumé of his accomplishments. What made it more than just a boring list were unusual tidbits of information scattered throughout. Part of the speech read:

> Obviously . . . Arnold is a huge movie star. As a result
> of his screen accomplishments he has been described
> by Time magazine as "arguably the global village's

most important star." His origins as a body building
champion gave him his start. He was a five time
Mr. Universe and seven time Mr. Olympia. He was
named chairman of the President's Council on Physical
Fitness. President Bush noted that he was the person
to raise the consciousness of all Americans to the
importance of health and physical fitness.

You can also discuss how the honoree got where he or she is. Did someone start out as a foreman and rise to CEO? In one case the speaker mentioned, "Jean is known as an Internet pioneer, although few realize she began as a journalist. She wrote for *Business Week* and moved on to CNN."

TUNE IN TO ISSUES SURROUNDING THE EVENT

New York State assemblyman Kevin Cahill was asked to make a tribute to someone honored by a local environmental group. The honoree was in the last stages of a serious illness. The occasion was a play staged to raise money for the organization, produced in part by the honoree's son and daughter.

In his tribute, Cahill focused on their participation, with "For all we know about————, and all the gifts he's given to the community in terms of public service, the greatest gift he gave us was creating two children who have a social conscience." He essentially said to the honoree, "Your work is done. You should be proud of yourself."

In a case like this, Cahill told me, "The difficulty is not so much in coming up with something to say; it's in the delivery of an emotional subject. Things may look perfectly good on paper and sound as if they should be easy to say. Yet at the moment you stand in front of a group, the emotions take control. That which is written may be far more difficult to deliver than it was to read."

WARM IT UP WITH PERSONAL INFORMATION

Include interesting details that humanize the honoree and might be news to the audience, as in, "Bill and his wife June just had triplets." Or, "It's common knowledge that Bill is a brilliant retailer, but he's also a lover of English literature. He reads Shakespeare to his wife Ginnie every night."

The Schwarzenegger tribute mentioned, "Arnold's commitment to family is another side of our honoree that many do not know. He loves everything about fatherhood, including getting up before sunrise to watch his newborn daughter get fed."

You can also comment on the person's many dimensions in life. An individual is not just a career description. He's a citizen, and may be a community leader, volunteer fireman, church member, and antique auto collector. You might say something like, "He dives head first into good causes. He's a Big Brother and serves on the boards of Clinton Hospital and the Holt Museum."

At the Democratic National Convention in Los Angeles in 2000, Tipper Gore framed her tribute around photographs she had taken of Vice President Albert Gore and their life together. It effectively communicated her husband's varied roles—politician, father, husband, son, even boyfriend.

Be flexible, too. If there is late-breaking news, comment on it, as in, "Little did we know when we asked George Simmons to be our honoree that he'd get an offer he couldn't refuse—the presidency of Southeastern College." (Or that he'd win the Pulitzer Prize or be named to a national commission.)

EMPLOYEE AWARDS AND TRIBUTES

Awards for achievement or for years of service send the message, "We know you're special." Recognition helps cement loyalty and encourage future accomplishment.

The president of a junior sportswear company honored the salesman of the year with: "Jeff consistently tops himself—and everyone else. This year he's opened new markets for us and brought in business we never expected. He doesn't know the meaning of the word *impossible*. For an outstanding sales record this year, I'm honored to present (name of award)."

Honoring the office manager's fifteenth year with a travel agency, the owner recalled hiring the person. The tribute said,

Some of us get lucky, and we've been among the fortunate, Gretchen, because we've got you. I remember the day you walked into my office for your interview. You were nervous, but your intelligence was

hard to miss. After the first five sentences out of your mouth, I knew you were just what we needed. Obviously I'm a stellar judge of people, because you've been an anchor for me and the whole organization. You're the coolest one here in a crisis. You just get better and better every year. So it is the greatest of pleasure that I present you with this pin in appreciation of your fifteenth anniversary with us.

Of course, you don't need an award to say thank you to a valued employee. A senior vice president in the beauty products industry honored an employee this way:

How does one describe two score years of devotion and loyalty? Two words: Claire Parker.

Claire is an icon in our industry. As one of America's foremost authorities on cosmetics, she has mentored students, chemists, and marketers alike. She has appeared on television and lectured at some of the most prestigious beauty events in New York, Boston, Chicago, and in Paris.

She has been an adviser and consultant to editors, authors, and leading cosmetologists, and has been referred to as The Walking Encyclopedia of Beauty Care. But it is not only her knowledge that makes her a leader and teacher. Her charismatic personality makes you want to learn and enjoy what you're learning. One of her students inscribed a book to her, "You are magic!" And she certainly is.

HOW TO ACCEPT AN AWARD

Keep your eye on the ball: the goal is to express sincere thanks. You don't want to sound phony, falsely modest, or sugary. On the other hand, you should also beware of coming across as arrogant. Get in touch with how you really feel about receiving the award. Elated? Humbled? Excited? Is it a tremendous validation of your work? Show it, as in, "I am awed and thrilled to receive this affirmation from my peers." People want to know that you appreciate the honor and that you feel it's important.

If there is anyone to thank (such as a mentor), do so. But limit yourself to a quick name or two—not a roster of fifty, which bores the audience and devalues the thanks. Your gratitude will seem false if it's shared with everyone including the janitor.

For many occasions you can keep your remarks very brief. But if you're facing a ballroom audience of five hundred, your speech probably needs to be a bit longer. (In any case, keep it under seven minutes.) In a formal situation, you can also talk about what the organization or the theme of the award (such as finding a cure for cancer) means to you and why. Or focus on what it means to others. You can also discuss the outlook for the future and what *you* plan to do on behalf of the cause or the industry. And, of course, remember to say "Thank you."

NINE

CONGRATULATIONS AND

OTHER CELEBRATIONS

*W*hen good things happen to your colleagues, it's an opportunity for applause. But each occasion varies in terms of what it means to the person, what's at stake, and the message you want to send. A promotion and a new business launch are both happy events, but the latter involves many risks. And a toast to an employee for two decades of service will differ from one to a client of twenty years. The tips that follow will help you identify goals and underlying issues, figure out what you want to say, and add insight to your toast or tribute.

PROMOTION TOASTS

Career advancement is a very big deal, and a good toast or tribute reflects that. It recognizes the accomplishment and publicly acknowledges that something important has occurred. The salute will be appreciated because most people don't hear praise very often. To say a few potent words, with or without raising a glass:

TALK ABOUT WHY THE PERSON DESERVES TO MOVE AHEAD IN HIS CAREER

Mention what led to the promotion, as in, "Ted, you're the man for this job. It's great to see you get it. You led the way to new online technology that set the industry on its ear. Congratulations."

Validate the person's performance with something like, "Good for you. What a great job you did on the Adams account. You turned their business around." Or, "His policies and vision increased volume twenty percent in the last quarter."

CITE WHAT'S SPECIAL ABOUT THE PERSON

Is he or she a rising star, or the youngest controller in the firm's history, or the third female partner to date? Say so.

One executive put it this way:

*What can you say about a man who astounds you
with all he knows? There are very few people in this
category and that's why you put them in the class of
a genius. Keith is one of them. He's a "nonstop" person.
It never occurs to him that he can't do something. He
just barrels ahead and starts solving the problem. He
says, "What do we have? What do we want? What are we
willing to commit?" That's the whole answer to success.
To Keith, our new senior vice president.*

Another slant: "Hal is known as a devastating poker player. He obviously puts his bluffing skills to good use in his negotiations. He's been a killer for us. Thank goodness he's on our side."

Or how about: "Charlotte is at her best when everyone else is saying it can't be done. She loves a challenge. And she's earned this advancement."

DISCUSS THE PERSON'S ABILITY TO PERFORM IN THE NEW POSITION

Express confidence in future success, as in: "You helped reinvent this company. You stayed on top of the changes in our business, and you managed those changes to take us to the top. There's no doubt you'll be outstanding in your leadership position."

Or try: "You're a manager of people and a rainmaker. You're going to be great." Or: "Since your forte is relationships with customers, you're unquestionably the best person for the position."

Wish the individual luck in the future, too, as in, "Beatrice, you hit a home run for us, and now the Los Angeles office is lucky to get you. Here's to success in your new position." Or, you can simply say, "Keep it up."

It's also useful to mention people with whom the individual will work. Someone toasted a colleague's promotion to vice president for labor relations with: "You're in charge of union negotiations now and I know you'll do an outstanding job. Ken's your boss, and you're two compatible guys. What a team you'll make."

CONSIDER YOUR RELATIONSHIP

If you're close to the person (and the setting is casual), you can say, if you wish, something like, "Atta boy, buddy. You earned your title!" If it's appropriate try, "I'm so proud of you and what you've achieved," or, "I respect what you've done," or, "I'm proud to have worked with you."

You can express positive feelings anytime as in, "I've always admired you, Rachel," or, "Pete, you are such a charismatic leader. I'd follow you anywhere."

If you don't know the honoree well, focus on how *others* feel about him or her. Quote a colleague of the person or say something like, "Ask Ron's employees what they think of him, and you'll hear, 'He's a fair man who has helped us work as a unit.'"

LIGHTEN UP

A little humor is welcome, as in, "Congratulations, Lucy, on your promotion to executive vice president. I never got to talk to you today. I couldn't get through. The whole world must have been calling to wish you well."

Someone kidded a coworker with: "I saw the announcement of your promotion in the newspaper. Your picture reminded me of a Wanted poster. Fortunately, you have other talents."

In very informal situations—such as the company picnic or champagne in paper cups in the office—if there is real affection for the person, it's okay to get silly. A middle manager created his own words to the song "You Are My Sunshine" and crooned to his newly promoted boss along with coworkers: "You're now our leader, the tops in our book." As always, keep it tasteful. No off-color jokes.

TOASTS FOR LAUNCHING A NEW BUSINESS

When someone starts a new venture, a lot is on the line—money, career, reputation. It's a step that takes courage. You want to congratulate the person, of course, but this is also a time to think about risk taking, because he or she is taking a chance. Express support and confidence in the endeavor's success and in the person's ability to attract new accounts. Talk about timing, as in, "The time is right for this kind of e-business. It fills a gap."

One executive, after being forced to leave her old position, started a consulting company. Within a few months, she had so much business, she was turning away clients. A friend toasted: "Here's to Edie Foster, who turned losing a job into the best thing that ever happened to her. Edie, six months ago you thought this was the end of your career. I guess it was—the end of *that* career. Today you are in such demand, you're raising your fees. You're an inspiration to us all."

TOASTS FOR OPENING A NEW OFFICE

Expansion means excitement, growth, and opportunity ahead. Offer congratulations and hopes for success in the new location. A CPA toasted a client: "Congratulations on your new presence in Boston. This is a smart move that will pay off big, I'm sure."

Or try: "I propose a toast to wish you success in your new office next year and in the future. To the Jones Company!"

When a matchmaking service announced the opening of its new headquarters in Denver, a supplier toasted, "Doctors, lawyers, and Indian chiefs had better watch out. You're going to get married. To everyone at The Dating Company!"

TOASTS FOR RELOCATING THE COMPANY

One company moved from Ohio to Texas to build business with South America. An attorney applauded with a toast: "This is a daring move, but one that is bound to open new markets. We raise our glasses to you." Another option: "Our headquarters is now where it belongs—in the heart of Silicon Valley."

You can also refer to characteristics of the new offices, as, "The view has certainly improved with those windows overlooking the Hudson instead of a brick wall." Is the new place more conveniently located, more spacious? Can you now get a parking space because there's a garage in the new office building? This is all material for your toast.

Is there anything you'll miss about the old place? Say, "I *will* miss lunch at George's Grill," and you'll probably get a laugh.

TOASTS FOR A JOB WELL DONE

Congratulating employees on winning new business or completing a project is an important kind of cheerleading. A pat on the back builds camaraderie and loyalty. In fact, there's a strong correlation between receiving approval and job satisfaction.

Let's say your advertising agency just won a huge account with $50 million in billings. How about a toast to those who participated in the winning presentation? This salutes everyone's effort and lays the foundation for working together again.

Says a creative director, You want to make everyone feel they made a major impact. Clearly some people did more than others, but the heavy hitters can't do *their* jobs without support staff doing their jobs. Every contribution, no matter how small, is important because there is a domino effect. If you have a great executive assistant, it means you don't have to worry about a lot of details you ordinarily would have to handle.

> *The people most affected are in the lower echelons.*
> *Once you reach a certain level, you're getting paid*

enough and have enough power so that it's not so
important to have cheerleaders. Obviously, everyone
wants to hear they did a good job, but it's more
important for some than others.

He tries to mention one or two people from each group by name. "It's about showmanship," he says, "but it's also about positioning people as family. The idea is, you're among friends instead of just doing your job."

In such a situation, you might say something like: "It was a great win for the agency, a seamless integration of all the departments. Everybody contributed. Congratulations to all of you. You should feel very proud."

You might also say, "There were no heroes in this pitch. Everyone stepped up to the plate and did a job above and beyond. No one person had to shoulder the whole burden. The feeling was that everybody was working so hard, no one wanted to let anyone else down—and it showed."

Or, "I knew coming out of the presentation that we'd won it. It was just a question of the client realizing how good we were. A lot of you had never worked with each other before. Units that don't ordinarily interact joined this time to win a client. But now I think you'll all be excited to do it again."

Cheerleading works in any company or profession when a difficult project has been completed. A packaged goods executive toasted his team, "The demands on everyone have been extraordinary this year. The wear and tear could have sunk us. Yet we've come through, stronger than ever. Here's to all of us."

When a scientist earned her Ph.D., a colleague acknowledged the investment involved with: "Helen, you've studied and slaved for this. Congratulations!"

At a catalog company's Christmas party, a CEO toasted employees with: "Plenty of firms are singing the blues these days. Not us. We've acquired another company and had a fantastic year. And we couldn't have done it without you. To Billings & Brown—and everyone here who makes it move."

Another option: "This would not have been possible without the hard work and tenacity of the invaluable Patricia King."

Whatever you say, do remember your goal and your audience. In one case, two companies were working together on a joint project for the first time. At a reception following a meeting, a top executive spontaneously jumped up on a table and offered a toast in the form of a drinking song. The words were well-meaning, but they had nothing whatever to do with the occasion; the song could have been sung anywhere, anytime. Although the speaker did tack on a brief mention of a "fruitful collaboration," it was a case of too little, too late. The toast fell flat.

Think how much more effective the toast could have been if it had focused on the joint effort. The speaker could have celebrated this first occasion to work together, and mentioned specific individuals by name. Challenges in the industry and common interests could have been discussed, as in, "We all face the demands of globalization, and we can benefit from sharing ideas and resources." It could have been a bonding experience for the participants, but instead just left people unmoved.

TOASTS FOR PROFESSIONAL ANNIVERSARIES

Success in business is built on interpersonal contact. The anniversary of a professional relationship is an opportunity to enhance ties with customers, suppliers, or others who are important to you.

On the tenth anniversary of a partnership between a big client, a broker, and a surety company, a surety executive used a strong anecdote to show his regard for the client. The tribute:

> *I am honored to be here tonight to celebrate the ten-year partnership between McCall's Company, Rand & Rand, and Underwriters United.*
>
> *There are several words that I can use to describe McCall's. Those words include* world class, first rate, cutting edge, *and* smart; *but my favorite word is* persistent.
>
> *The dictionary says to be persistent is to hold fast and firm to a purpose despite obstacles. There have been many cases over the last ten years where McCall's could have been labeled persistent, but there is no example better than the time about five years ago when Bob Northridge instructed Jerry Bolton to plant himself in my office until I approved one particular bond. Poor Jerry sat there in my office for four days. He would arrive in the office shortly after I arrived in the morning. He left the office in the*

evening when I was done for the day. Finally, I could
not take him any longer. I had to approve the bond.

That's what you call persistence! Tonight, I am
proud and honored to salute the fine people of
McCall's and our ten years together.

Someone else toasted a longer relationship: "We are here tonight to celebrate a business partnership that began twenty years ago. I am particularly proud to have been your adviser and friend for all these years. Here's to the successes of the past—and to many profitable years ahead."

Every client wants to feel appreciated, and this toast by a partner in an architectural firm was right on target: "We've been working together for fifteen years, and we want you to know how much we appreciate your business, your loyalty, and your confidence. All of these things mean a great deal to us."

Another toast told a customer that he was valued for his friendship, as well as his orders: "Over the years, our relationship has become more than just a business."

Sometimes the client feels the same way about you, as in this toast to an attorney:

We so often get wrapped up in the details of life and
lose sight of those things that are truly important,
such as telling our friends just how much they mean to
us. With that in mind, I want to take this opportunity
to thank you, Rick, for your friendship, counsel, and
support. I appreciate all that you do, not only for me,

but for all the employees of this company. You are a treasure.

When I first began to work with you, you used to intimidate me, simply because you knew so much, and you were so assertive in your presentations. I have since come to understand that this gruffness is a facade, nothing more than an actor's role in playing his part, and that you are actually a very caring individual with a heart of gold. For that I am also grateful. I am fortunate to have you as a friend.

Another client made this toast: "We've all heard lawyer jokes, but Sid breaks the mold. Many of his clients wind up becoming his friends. His uncommon good sense and infectious wit, not to mention his brilliant legal mind, is a package that is irresistible."

Of course, you don't need an anniversary to celebrate a relationship. President John F. Kennedy did so in his tribute to the Australian and U.S. crews in the America's Cup race in 1962. Speaking of the long friendship between the two countries, he said,

We have the highest regard for Australia. . . . [We] regard them as very satisfactory friends in peace, and the best of friends in war. And I know there are a good many Americans of my generation who have the greatest possible reason to be grateful to the Australians who wrote a most distinguished record all the way from the desert of North Africa, and most particularly in the islands of the South Pacific, where

> *their particular courage and gallantry I think met the*
> *strongest response in all of us in this country.*

These moving remarks, at a dinner given by the Australian ambassador to the United States, elicit a strong response even decades later.

Obviously, not all celebratory toasts are so grand in scale. At an ordinary dinner, a toast to a valued business associate might say, "To Liz. If only all of life went as smoothly as our projects together. Here's to more of them ahead."

You don't need to be fancy or clever, either. Raising a glass to a customer and his wife, one stockbroker toasted, "To Jane and Harold, two terrific people whom it has been my pleasure to know." It wasn't elaborate, but it was very nice to hear.

TEN

WELCOMES AND GOOD-BYES

$\mathscr{A}$ warm reception is common courtesy when someone joins or visits your organization, and so is a heartfelt farewell when someone leaves to pursue a new opportunity. Welcome toasts can ease a newcomer's entry, create a friendly atmosphere, and encourage sociability. They also work well when you meet with government officials, colleagues from other branches of your office, or representatives of other companies. On the flip side, toasts can be a thoughtful way to say farewell when a co-worker leaves to take another job, start a new venture, or change careers.

WELCOME TOASTS

Say a few words to set the stage for a positive working relationship with a new employee or coworker. It means a great deal to newcomers to feel enthusiastically received by their employer and colleagues.

Since you probably don't know the new person well in this situation, focus on how he or she will contribute to the company. Mention previous experience as in, "Burt's innovative approaches to e-commerce doubled sales at Roberts & Blanchard. He's about to implement a bunch of programs here at Gruening Inc., and we're excited to help him make them happen. Let's welcome Burt Arnett, our new director of sales." Or try, "Bill's ideas at Calgore Inc., attracted customers to their web site. He's got big plans for our web site, too. Let's give him all the help we can."

You can also discuss the specific need filled by the person, as in, "We reached outside the industry to get Ann. She broadens our management ranks, and based on her past performance, she's going to broaden our profits as well." Or how about, "Ray is known for launching the successful research department that traced customer buying patterns for Bates & Co. We need to strengthen our research, and he will fill an important gap for us."

If you wish, you can add some background to personalize your toast, as in, "Joe has not only been a business leader, he also quietly pays back to the community. He's been an enthusiastic volunteer paramedic for ten years." This kind of information also helps trigger conversations with the newcomer. After the toast, people are likely to walk up to him and say things like, "I've always wanted to be a volunteer paramedic or fireman," or inquire "How many hours a week are you on duty?"

If it fits, mention a trend, as in, "Local online advertising is expected to double in the next two years, which is why we're so excited about Jim's move here. His track record proves he can get a big slice of that pie."

Other possibilities include:

"Please welcome Harry Peters. Nobody knows the industry better and we're fortunate to have his wisdom and experience."

Or, "Sharon adds class and experience to our operation. We're lucky to have her. Welcome, Sharon."

Or, "I'm sure most of you already know Frank. For you younger people who may not, here are some highlights of his distinguished career."

Or, "Let's welcome James Rootan. He has years of experience growing profits at Rogers Corporation. Now he's going to do the same for us."

Or, "Join me in a toast to Larry, who will supervise all of our U.S. operations and execute our strategic business plan. He brings with him over fifteen years of experience."

Or, "Welcome Richard Riley, our new regional VP of operations, who reports to Bob Kendall. Rich handled daily operations in Florida and same store sales jumped thirty percent during his tenure. We look forward to his experience and expertise benefiting the whole southern region." These kinds of introductions provide important support to the newcomer.

Sometimes you must introduce a visiting official or supplier, or an employee from another division. Help the visitor feel at home and among friends who are happy to see him. Identify the person's connection and include praise when possible. Guests remember your kindness.

You might also say something like, "It's a pleasure to have with us tonight John Henderson of our Omaha office. It was John who worked so successfully with Congress on the new legislation. Welcome to Chicago, John."

When welcoming visitors from another country, it's a nice touch to toast in their language, as in, *"Salud"* (Mexico), *"Sköal"* (Scandinavian), *"Na zdorov'e"* (Russian), *"Slainte"* (Ireland), or *"Prosit"* (Germany).

FAREWELL TOASTS

When someone is moving away after a transfer or leaving the company for another job, he or she won't be around on a daily basis anymore. Good-byes are hard to do, but they're also a chance to recount the good times and reminisce about the challenges you faced together. In a toast or tribute, you can use many of the tips suggested for retirement. Talk about what you'll miss most about the person, as in, "I'll miss walking into your office to brainstorm ideas." Or, "I'll miss your loud ties and your daily recap of the football scores." Lament, "Who will run the baseball pool this summer?" or, "Who will orchestrate the office Christmas party?" or, "Who will help me figure out all my computer glitches?"

Talk about how much the company will miss the person for either a casual or a more formal tone, or if you don't have personal anecdotes. When her boss transferred to another office, an administrator toasted, "Everybody loves you—even former employees. They buy you Christmas presents and keep coming back to have lunch with you. Well, now you'll have to take *me* to lunch! Here's wishing you the best."

Someone delivered this tribute to a colleague transferred a continent away:

> *You've been a role model for younger associates and you've charted a course for those of us who are not so young. That's not to say there haven't been setbacks or problems, but it's been a privilege to be part of your successful tenure here.*
>
> *Thank you for being my colleague and my friend and making my years working with you so memorable. Our loss is the Hong Kong office's gain. I plan to stay in touch, and hope you won't forget us anymore than we will forget you.*

Another tribute went, "If there is a better marketing manager in the United States, I haven't met him. You've set a standard that others in our industry seek to emulate. Now that you're moving on to your next challenge, there's no doubt you'll excel once again."

Someone offered this toast to an executive leaving to launch his own consulting company: "Len has been a key member of our management team, and he is widely admired throughout the industry. We wish him success in his new venture, but he will be sorely missed."

You can compare the company's success before and after the person arrived, as in, "When Dan joined Davidson Hardware, his biggest problem was our declining market share. Now that's a barely remembered bad dream. Today we've got eighty percent of the market, thanks to his creativity and successful strategies. You leave us in good shape, Dan." Or try something like, "We were hit hard by customer complaints until you arrived to launch our new system. What a difference it made. What a difference *you* made, Ed. You're irreplaceable."

Sometimes the departure involves the president of a professional or charitable organization, or the chairperson of an important committee who has completed a term. A colleague made this tribute to a veteran committee member: "June has been on the conference committee for ten long years and she's had about enough. *We'll* never have enough of her leadership and energy, however."

When a task force head left one nonprofit organization, her successor's farewell tribute focused on her leadership style:

Today we are here to honor Norma Smith, who has been our chair for the last three years. And what a superb job she has done. All of us have learned from Norma. She has set an example in getting rid of the word but and substituting the word and. It is never, "I see your point, but . . ." It is, "I see your point, and . . ." That simple word has paved the way toward agreement in all the decisions of our task force.

Norma has encouraged honest feedback from us, while knowing that sometimes feedback is a risk. The two words that keep popping up when I think about her are trust and caring.

What Norma has done is the following: She trusted us on the front end and never withheld that trust. She cared. She was always consistent. We all knew that she could be counted on because she eliminated discrepancies between what was said and what was done. She cared. She always listened with an open mind and respected other opinions, because she knew that every opinion was worth hearing even if there was disagreement. She cared. If a mistake was made, she was there to correct it. No buck was ever passed, because she cared. Last, she always gave credit where credit was due. She had her team and recognized everyone. All because she cared—and we all know she always will. Norma has been a great chair, a wonderful leader, a creative mind and a terrific friend.

These words honored the outgoing president of a professional organization:

Ted came to this job at a time of turmoil for the organization. Some of us wondered if it would survive the warring factions. Yet Ted united us, calmed us down, and quietly yet firmly steered us toward the future. A lot of people think strength is a loud voice. Ted shows us that strength is calm maturity, thoughtful consideration of issues, fairness, and the ability to work for the good of the entire organization.

I applaud you, Ted. You're a leader with heart. You inspired confidence and pulled us together. We'll miss you more than you know.

Good-bye toasts don't always have to be serious or sentimental, especially if the people involved appreciate workplace humor. When the president of a trade association had served his term, some members took a light approach. Alluding to the frustrations of the job (even mentioning people he had worked with), they kidded him at an informal party with this rhyme recited in unison:

Can it be true
That four years have passed?
Who was it that said,
"You certainly won't last"?

Well, here you are
After all this time,
Not wiser, just older,
With a marked stoop in the shoulder.

But it must be said
That alone you were not:
There were Kathy and Betty,
Always there on the dot;
Harold and Peter were on this road;
And Stuart and George
Helped carry the load.

So, adieu, Mr. Mike,
You have served us quite well;
The time has now come
To sound the final bell.
But before we close
On this your last hail,
We want you to know,
Your check's in the mail!

ELEVEN

RETIREMENTS

$\mathscr{R}$etirement is a transition that stirs our emotions. It's often tinged with mixed feelings—sadness *and* smiles. It leads us to take stock of someone else's work life, and in the process, ponder our own plans for the future. For all of these reasons, a good toast or tribute takes some thought. Whether the retiree is a clerk or CEO, the tips on the following pages will help you clarify what's going on and say something that matters.

SUM UP ACHIEVEMENTS

You want to salute the accomplishments of a lifetime. One option is to start with a relevant quote, as in, "Publius Syrus said, 'Anyone can steer the ship when the sea is calm.' Mark is a leader for the storms."

You can also discuss the person's impact on the company or industry, as in, "Visionaries are few and far between, but Vince is the genuine article. His commitment to innovation and excellence has led us to unequaled growth in the last twenty years. He leaves us strong—a tight, efficient organization that gets results and knows how to work as a team. We have all been touched by his tenure."

Or try something like, "What can you say about forty-one years of dedicated, creative leadership? Well, you can point to the tenfold increase in employees and the string of successful acquisitions."

What if the retiree is not a star, but simply an employee who does his job? Reliability and loyalty over the long haul deserve praise. These days, working for the same company for thirty years is an accomplishment in itself.

The executive director of a nonprofit used the theme "Josie is the heart of the department," and then illustrated why that was so, saying, "She's been here longer than any of us and cares deeply about this firm and about all of us. I want everyone to know she is leaving, because she's probably too shy to tell you herself and she deserves this recognition."

BE SENSITIVE TO CIRCUMSTANCES

Before you say, "How wonderful, now you can sleep late," consider the situation. Although some people can hardly wait to leave, others feel different. Someone forced into retirement, gently or otherwise, may view the future as less than appealing. In such a case, focus on a show of support and expressions of admiration. Mention how much you're looking forward to continued future contact, as in, "We'll be expecting you at our regular Tuesday lunch."

Talk about how the person will be missed, as in, "The company won't be the same without you," or, "What are we going to do without you?" Such sentiments also resonate when retirement is eagerly anticipated, but they are especially welcome if the person isn't thrilled to leave.

EXPLORE WHO THE PERSON IS

Does he or she have people skills or organizational ability? Say, "When we had late delivery problems, you solved them, just as you dealt with excess inventory. Who can fill your shoes?" Or, "You set tough goals and then inspired us to do the impossible. You cut red tape to help us get mountains out of our way."

Anecdotes and memories can offer glimpses of personality, as in this tribute to a consultant by a former employee: "When something would go wrong I remember Mr. Cabot would say, 'You're a turkey.' One day he started clucking. Another time he bought candy corn and spread it around my desk."

Another speaker recalled, "Sheila has always been a real character and a great fund-raiser. I once asked her for advice on fund-raising pitches, and she told me the secret of her speeches. She said, 'If you're short and dumpy like me, you've got to do something to get their attention.' She did just that, telling incredible stories to audiences—and she got them to give more than they expected to."

Someone toasted an accountant: "Don, you have really been an employment agency. You matched so many clients with business deals that benefited them. You hired so many friends when they needed work. Everyone knows that when you're in trouble, you go to Don. Well, you're finally getting a well-deserved rest. Here's to you."

TALK ABOUT WHAT'S NEXT

Retirement marks the end of a career and lifestyle and the beginning of something else. In the past, it meant the start of a life of leisure, leavened perhaps by a hobby, volunteer work, or travel. Today, retirement is often a transition to a new kind of occupation. Is there something important the retiree wants to do, such as enter politics, teach, or write a novel? Pep up your speech with the information, as in, "I know you're itching to get back to school to finally get your degree."

The person may be retiring only to turn around and start a whole new career or business. A coworker toasted a petroleum engineer who specialized in safety programs, "Cal, you're retiring on Friday and opening your new consulting business on Monday. So we'll no doubt be hearing a lot about you. Here's to your next life."

When a fashion manufacturer retired to head a medical research foundation, his former partner toasted, "Jim, you never *could* resist a challenge. To important breakthroughs."

A lawyer made this tribute to a business associate who retired at fifty-nine:

Abe, you're much too young to pack it in. You've said that you want to spend time tinkering with your many computers and your collection of antique toys. I know you want to try photography. But you also mentioned other mysterious plans, and I suspect that it won't be long before you surprise us. We'll miss you, old buddy, but we also await your next incarnation. Best of luck!

If you're stuck for ideas, use a retirement gift as the trigger for your speech. In one case a company gave the person a gift certificate for higher education. Coworkers gleefully toasted, "Good luck in school! We won't help you with your homework."

When the owner of a food distribution company turned over the reins to his sons, industry colleagues presented him with some carpentry equipment. Said a spokesman in his speech, "Al, we thought it was time to get that workshop you've been dreaming about. So we pooled our resources for this gift."

Someone else said, "Great leaders don't come along every day. It's been a privilege to hang around and absorb your knowledge. We wish you the best in your new life ahead."

You can also try a quote as in, "Robert Frost said, 'By working faithfully eight hours a day, you may eventually get to be boss and work twelve hours a day.' Your hours were a lot longer than that, Ben. Enjoy your new freedom."

GET PERSONAL

Warmth is critical in a retirement tribute because everyone expects to hear expressions of affection or gratitude. A tribute to a retiring vice president went:

> *You've made an indelible impression on this company and on me personally. You always expected the highest level of performance from me. Sometimes I didn't think I could live up to those expectations. But I usually did, thanks to your faith and trust in me. You motivated me and others to do our best.*
>
> *I'll never forget the way you sat down and discussed my future with me, listening rather than lecturing, and ultimately giving me wise advice. When I moved out of the department into a new position, you always kept tabs on me and wanted to know how I was doing. Neither I—nor anyone else here—is ready to see you go.*

Someone else toasted:

> *I've observed and learned from you for the past six years. You've been a role model par excellence. I've*

*always been astonished at your ability not only to
make decisions, but to make the right decisions.*

*You've told me that life is short, and you've decided
to live accordingly and follow your star to a new life
with your family. I and everyone else here wish you
happiness in that pursuit. Here's to you, Matt.*

You can also use a list of thank-yous as a device, as in, "Thank you for teaching me everything you know about market research. Thank you for refusing to listen to the pundits. Thank you for telling me quirky jokes every day, which always made the office fun. Thank you for your sound judgment."

Or consider wordplay where it fits. In remarks on the retirement of a state senator named Grace, an official said, "The word *grace* is defined as a disposition to be generous, helpful, and to have goodwill. Thank you for your grace in politics, your grace of character, and your grace of person. And thank you for your courage to break gender barriers and to show the next generation of women how to lead in today's world."

When a packaging executive retired early, a former employee made this tribute:

*Fred, this is an industry where mentors stand out. And
few stand out bolder than you do. You've helped so
many of us, who are now succeeding in companies
throughout the world, thanks to your guidance and
encouragement.*

*I am fortunate to have been one of your protégés,
having trained under your wing. I regret that future*

*leaders will not have that benefit. Thank you for the
enormous impact you've had on my own growth and
on the entire business we're in. I wish you the best of
luck in your future plans.*

Are you praising a retiree with whom you've had a less than ideal
relationship? A middle manager turned that truth into a powerful tribute:

*Dave, I must admit that I envy your decision to retire
and spend more time with your family. It's hard to
envision you moving at less than breakneck speed,
and you've already mentioned projects you've got on
the back burner.*

*It's been a privilege to work with you, and I have
grown as a result. In retrospect, I wish we had been
able to work even closer. I think now of opportunities
missed on my part and I regret them, for you are one
terrific manager and mentor. I admire you more than
I can say. Thanks for eight years of great experience
and learning.*

GET CREATIVE

When a beloved administrator retired after twenty-one years at
a nonprofit, a coworker organized a tribute. Starting months in
advance, she purchased a memory book in a stationery store,
then gathered information to fill it. Polling every department,

she asked, "What are her favorite things?" The answers included Mickey Mouse, chocolates, Yorkshire terriers, and cookbooks, so the coworkers decorated the pages of the memory book with stickers and pictures inspired by these interests. Because the retiree played three different instruments, stickers of musical notes also appeared.

Individual friends contributed pages of their memories. Because the retiree and a coworker called each other "Thelma and Louise," one page featured a picture of the movie poster. Relevant articles about her from the company newsletter were also reproduced for the book.

On the day she retired, the album was presented at her surprise party. The organizer explained in her tribute: "When we asked each department to say something about you, there was no loss for words. We were overwhelmed with the contributions. We had to buy extra pages for the book. It's a testimony to who you are. You can be sure you're going to be missed." A keepsake to cherish, the book proclaimed just how special people thought she was.

Others prefer poetry at a time like this. One selection targeted a retiring New York State transportation executive. It was composed and read at an industry meeting by a colleague:

> *We traveled to L.A. to bid you adieu,*
> *And in Key Largo, we said good-bye too;*
> *We listened to speeches*
> *On the Florida beaches,*

Even heard tales of your plans
To go to faraway lands.

And now your friends are at it anew,
Yet another party to share some brew;
Since it's a gala for you, I'm inclined to say Yes,
The invite reply is not hard to guess;
The reason, my friend, that I chose to say No,
Is, even for you, I don't do Buffalo!

CONSIDER SHORT TAKES

Sometimes you simply want to make a brief, casual toast. Try something like, "We took a vote in our department and decided you're the best boss we ever had. Here's to you." Or, "Some people would be happy with *ten* good years with a company. Bernie has had *thirty-five* years, all of them good. Here, here!"

Or, "You're going to be a hard act to follow. Time passes too quickly. We raise our glasses in your honor. Here's to you!"

APPENDIX

SOME LONGER TOASTS

AND TRIBUTES

SEPTEMBER 14, 1962, NEWPORT, R.I.

I know that all of us take the greatest pleasure in being here, first of all because whether we are Australian or American, we are all joined by a common interest, a common devotion and love for the sea, and I am particularly glad to be here because this Cup is being challenged by our friends from Australia, this extraordinary group of men and women numbering some 10 million, who have demonstrated on many occasions, on many fields, in many countries, that they are the most extraordinary athletic group in the world today, and that this extraordinary demonstration of physical vigor and skill has come not by the dictates of the state, because the Australians are among the freest citizens in the world, but because of their choice.

Therefore, Ambassador, you are most welcome here.

This Cup has been challenged in the past by our friends from Great Britain. We are glad to see Australia assuming the responsibilities of empire in coming here, and we are particularly glad to welcome you in the year 1962. This is a trophy which the United States has held for over a century, unlike the Davis Cup. And we do have a feeling, Ambassador, we do have an old American motto of "One cup at a time."

There is no question that this kind of national competition

produces the greatest goodwill among nations. The most recent indication of that, of course, were the games held at Indonesia which produced a wonderful feeling of spirit in all of Asia, and I am confident that these games will produce the same kind of goodwill between Australia and the United States.

I really don't know why it is that all of us are so committed to the sea, except I think it is because in addition to the fact that the sea changes and the light changes, and ships change, it is because we all came from the sea. And it is an interesting biological fact that all of us have, in our veins, the exact same percentage of salt in our blood that exists in the ocean, and therefore, we have salt in our blood, in our sweat, in our tears.

We are tied to the ocean. And when we go back to the sea, whether it is to sail or to watch it, we are going back from whence we came.

Therefore, it is quite natural that the United States and Australia, separated by an ocean, but particularly those of us who regard the ocean as a friend, bound by an ocean, should be meeting today in Newport to begin this great sea competition. This is an old relationship between the United States and Australia, and particularly between Rhode Island and Australia.

In the 1790s, Ambassador, American ships, mostly from Rhode Island, began to call regularly at New South Wales. Their cargoes, I regret to say, consisted mainly of gin and rum, and the effect was to set back the athletic development, until the recent great temperance movement in Australia, for many years.

In 1801, Governor Philip Gidley King, of Australia, complained to London, "Such has been the certainty in America of any quantity of spirits being purchased here, that a ship cleared out of Rhode Island for this port with a very large investment of spirits, which I positively forbade being landed, in consequence of which she left this port with upward of 13,000 gallons of spirit brought to Australia for sale." And he told the American minister Rufus King to warn the Rhode Island merchants not to try to market their rum in Australia. I need hardly say that the Rhode Island merchants continued to do their compassionate best to quench the thirst which was felt so strongly in Australia.

However, Australia became committed to physical fitness and it has been disastrous for the rest of us. We have the highest regard for Australia, Ambassador. As you said, we regard them as very satisfactory friends in peace, and the best of friends in war. And I know there are a good many Americans of my generation who have the greatest possible reason to be grateful to the Australians who wrote a most distinguished record all the way from the desert of North Africa, and most particularly in the islands of the South Pacific, where their particular courage and gallantry I think met the strongest response in all of us in this country.

But I really don't look to the past. I look to the present. The United States and Australia are most intimately bound together today, and I think that—and I speak as one who has had some experience in friendship and some experience in those who are not our friends—we value very much the fact that on the other side of the Pacific the Australians inhabit a very key and crucial area, and that the United States is most intimately associated with them. So beyond this race, beyond the result, rests this happy relationship between two great people.

I want to toast tonight the crew, the sailors, those who made it possible for the *Gretel* to come here, those who have, for a hundred years, defended this Cup from the New York Yacht Club, to all of them. As the Ambassador said so well, they race against each other, but they also race with each other against the wind—and the sea. To the crew of the *Gretel* and the crew of the *Weatherly*.

WEDDING REHEARSAL DINNER TOAST, BY DR. ROBERT BOXER

First, I want to welcome you all to the "dinner the night before." We have people here tonight from a huge diversity of locations, including Oregon, California, Florida, Louisiana, Iowa, Virginia, Connecticut, Maryland, New York City, Upstate New York, and of course Colombia and Chile, South America. I want to thank you all for coming to honor Cary and Bill. Some of the people here tonight have known Cary for a very long time and have met Bill on only a few occasions; others, the truly lucky ones in this room, have known them since they first began dating almost six and a half years ago and have witnessed the growth of their relationship. I am blessed to be one of those people.

The first time I met Cary was when Bill brought her to my apartment on their first date. They went to see *Schindler's List*. Although Bill introduced Cary as a "friend" from school, I knew later on when we all went out to dinner and Bill put his arm around Cary to protect her from the frigid New York cold that Cary was indeed much more than a casual friend.

I have so many wonderful memories of my son and Cary through those six and a half years that it's really hard to select a few to share with you. What I've chosen to do is to share my Father's Day memories with you.

Father's Day '94 they were on break from medical school— probably the last luxury of this type they will ever have. Bill had his bachelor pad apartment in Soho, New York City, with chums from both his college and high school days, all of whom will be here tomorrow to share his joy at the wedding. Cary and Bill met me for brunch at a French/Vietnamese restaurant in Soho. Both of them showed up wearing khaki shorts and sandals. Over her T-shirt Cary was wearing Bill's favorite Ralph Lauren madras shirt. I knew if Bill lent this shirt to anyone (something that had never happened before), this was indeed a very special person in his life. Cary had taken this men's extra-large shirt and draped and tied it around her so that it looked incredibly chic, in the inimitable way Cary has of making anything she puts on look wonderful.

Father's Day of their junior year, Cary and Bill had a wedding to attend in New Jersey. Cary was part of the bridal party, so Bill drove her out and then came back to New York to spend a few hours with me. This was a particularly difficult time in my life. I had just sold an apartment on Riverside Drive where I had lived for almost twenty years and had the day before signed a contract on a new apartment in Manhattan. I was very anxious for Bill to see my new apartment. Bill, of course, being the wonderful, sensitive young man that he is, drove in to see the apartment and take me to brunch. Afterward we sat in the park and had a wonderful talk before he drove back to New Jersey to join Cary at the wedding. I thought to myself what a lucky father I was to have a son like this.

Father's Day of their senior year was after their graduation from medical school, which was a totally joyous experience for all of us. At the same time Bill and Cary were coming to grips with their forthcoming internships in separate cities.

Once again the three of us spent the whole weekend together. Most of Saturday was spent shopping for things for Bill's new apartment in Boston. On Sunday we met for our customary Father's Day brunch at our favorite haunt on the Upper West Side—Ocean Grill. Again a beautiful weekend, exquisite weather and ideal company.

Last year—Father's Day 1999 and the final memory I'll share with you this evening.

I had spent a week in Florida helping my mom move. I returned late Friday, expecting to spend part of Saturday with Bill, and there was a message on my answering machine from Bill saying that because of his work schedule he would have to drive back and forth from Boston in one day. I discouraged this, and although somewhat disappointed at the prospect of spending Father's Day alone, I was fine with it. Cary was scheduled to work the whole weekend. An hour later Cary called and invited me to dinner. Although her work schedule was the same or worse than Bill's that weekend, at least she was in New York. We decided on a small Italian restaurant on the Upper East Side.

I arrived early or Cary was late, I don't remember. I was seated facing the door and when Cary entered that restaurant all eyes turned, men and women alike. She was so beautiful! I felt so proud to be with her as she bent and kissed me on the cheek.

Once again it was a wonderful meal, and Cary presented me with a turquoise shell shaving set from her and Bill, along with a card. Moments later she reached in her purse and pulled out another card and said, "This is from me alone."

The note read and I quote: "Dearest Bob, Thank you so much for your loving and caring ways. I feel as if the void that was left when my dad died in 1993 is filled now that you are part of my life."

I was overwhelmed! I felt that now, not only did I have an incredibly wonderful son, but a daughter as well.

I raise this glass to toast the two of you—to the wonderful, long, and happy marriage that I know you will enjoy because of the three most impressive traits you possess:

1. The love that is so evident in your relationship and which you so generously share with your family and friends.
2. Your accomplishments, which are far too numerous to go into here.
3. And last, your passion for life, which defines who you are and which I feel privileged to be a part of.

I love you both so much.

APRIL 14, 1997

Our guest of honor tonight, Arnold Schwarzenegger, is the embodiment of tireless dedication. It is our good fortune that his efforts are not limited to those of his accomplishments that are well-known. The general public is obviously aware of the fact that Arnold is a huge movie star. As a result of his screen accomplishments, he has been described by *Time* magazine as "arguably the global village's most important star." His origins as a body-building champion gave him his start. He was a five-time Mr. Universe and seven-time Mr. Olympia. He was named chairman of the President's Council on Physical Fitness. President Bush noted that he was the person to raise the consciousness of all Americans to the importance of health and physical fitness.

What's less well-known about our honoree is that Arnold is a prime example of someone who has raised his own sensitivities and consciousness. He has a passion for the Center's valued principles: remembrance, tolerance, truth, and hope. He has been a major contributor and fund-raiser. He's done so for some time; this is nothing new. Years ago Arnold got involved in the Center, and was among the first of the Hollywood stars to do so. He was well ahead of his time and certainly has done this without a great deal of recognition. He has raised awareness in the non-Jewish community and most importantly has made a commitment to ensure that this dedication of principles will continue not only through the next generation but for generations to come.

It's important to recognize that his dedication doesn't end with his personal contribution. Arnold's commitment to family is another side of our honoree that many do not know. He loves everything about fatherhood, including getting up before sunrise to watch his newborn daughter get fed.

The inscription of this award says the following: "The National Leadership Award is presented to Arnold Schwarzenegger in gratitude for his tireless efforts in helping to further the goals of the Simon Wiesenthal Center and the Museum of Tolerance." Ladies and gentlemen, our guest of honor, Arnold Schwarzenegger.

REFERENCE LIBRARY

Baldridge, Letitia. *Letitia Baldridge's New Complete Guide to Executive Manners*. New York: Rawson Associates, 1993.

Bartlett, John. *Bartlett's Familiar Quotations*. 16th ed. Justin Kaplan, ed. Boston: Little, Brown, 1992.

Byrne, Robert, comp. *1,911 Best Things Anybody Ever Said*. New York: Fawcett Columbine, 1988.

Cohl, H. Aaron, ed. *The Friars Club Encyclopedia of Jokes*. New York: Black Dog/Leventhal, 1997.

Dianda, Gretchen B., and Betty J. Hofmayer. *Older & Wiser*. New York: Ballantine Books, 1995.

Ehrlich, Eugene. *Amo, Amas, Amat and More*. New York: Harper & Row, 1985.

Lieberman, Gerald F. *3,500 Good Quotes for Speakers*. New York: Main Street/Doubleday, 1983.

Post, Elizabeth L. *Emily Post's Etiquette*. 15th ed. New York: HarperCollins, 1997.

The Quotable Woman. Philadelphia: Running Press, 1991.

Tripp, Rhoda Thomas, comp. *The International Thesaurus of Quotations*. New York: Harper & Row, 1970.

Winokur, Jon, comp. *The Portable Curmudgeon*. New York: NAL Books, 1987.

INDEX